MW01199506

Hey!

Thanks for being a guest on the radio show! You rock!

Your friend,

STAND UP & STAND OUT

AND WATCH YOUR PRODUCT FLY OFF THE STORE SHELVES

E. DAVID MARINAC

To Emily, Spencer,
and Susan (my original Angel)

Stand Up & Stand Out
And Watch Your Product Fly Off the Store Shelves

© 2015 E. David Marinac

Published by Voxie Media
Big Ideas. Short Books™

voxiemedia.com

No part of this book may be reproduced or transmitted in any form or by any means, graphic, electronic or mechanical, including photocopying, recording, taping or by any information storage and retrieval system, without the permission of the publisher.

ISBN 978-0-9861255-0-8
eISBN 978-0-9861255-1-5

Cover and interior design: Melanie Shellito of Artezen, LLC
Copyediting: Barbara McNichol and Tim Lawrence

PRAISE FOR *STAND UP & STAND OUT*

"An excellent primer for anyone wanting to know how to navigate the dangerous waters of sourcing from China."

— *Daryl Z. Todd, president of International Merchandise Group Asia and former VP of Asian Sourcing for Kmart*

"In this quick and powerful read, David Marinac divulges the secret ingredients to getting your products to fly off the shelves."

— *Jonathan B. Smith, founder and CEO of Chief Optimizer and former COO of Wave Dispersion Technologies*

CONTENTS

CHAPTER 1:

THE UNDERDOGS

Everybody loves an underdog. Whether it's the little kid standing up to the big bully or a version of the biblical David versus Goliath story, people relate to underdogs. Maybe at one time or another you've been an underdog—or can be called one now in your business arena.

All areas of business have underdogs, including the world of retail. That's right: While Walmart, Target, Whole Foods, and Costco could be considered the giants in retail, numerous smaller regional companies—even your local grocer—must find a way to beat these big boys. It's played out every day.

Regardless of whether your retail product pertains to food or to laundry detergent, pet treats, or vitamins, every company has to be prepared to "do battle" to first get on a store shelf, and in order to keep that hallowed position on the shelf, a product needs to sell, plain and simple.

The largest companies in the world can have the finest distribution networks, the best salespeople, and a world-class pricing/profit model, but at the end of the day, if their product doesn't sell, it's done. Toast.

Yes, your company can offer the best-tasting, longest-lasting, good-for-you item, but if no buyers know about it, then it will face its demise.

And knowing the old adage "a first impression is the most important," what happens in the retail world? If a product makes it onto a store shelf but doesn't have a "hot button"—something that says "pick me up and take me home"—before long, that product will be gone, banished to obscurity.

Changing Retail Climate Gives Underdogs a Chance

Yet over the past ten years, the retail landscape has changed. Local grocers don't have the clout or power they once did. Major retailers with their sophisticated inventory, replenishment systems, and ability to trim costs to maximize profits have swallowed smaller stores in many markets.

With that in mind, it would be logical to assume this trend would continue with the sale of products themselves. That means if you had an awesome product but weren't aligned with a big distributor like Procter & Gamble or Hartz or Nestlé, it would be doomed.

But something strange has happened in the retail climate. Some big retailers are featuring amazing products produced by independent companies that aren't affiliated with the "big boy" distributors. Lo and behold, they've given these innovative products a spot on their shelves.

Even more importantly, given the chance, these products have sold and sold very well—often for a premium price over what the major brands offered.

Bullying Tactics from the "Big Boys"

Yes, specialty versions and flavors of such basic items as cereal and granola, coffee and tea, even dog treats and protein powder are taking up store shelves. As you can imagine, the "big boys" didn't take kindly to these new upstarts, so they have attempted to silence them. Some have threatened to pull their products while others have grouped multiple items into "special offers" with additional profits for retailers — On the condition that that particular upstart product is no longer carried. Other conglomerates got creative. They created "jumbo" packs or spent R&D dollars to add an exclusive pour spout, specialty zip-lock, or other feature to make their products more appealing to consumers.

What's the one oft-overlooked thing that can make or break a product's success on a retail store shelf? If you guessed packaging, you'd be right.

Packaging Itself as the Underdog

Packaging can be considered an underdog that plays second fiddle to snazzy ingredients with cool-sounding names like "wild crafted bamboo extract" or "organic sprouted whole grain brown rice protein." While many consumers only see a package's exterior—how it looks or the colors it features—a lot has to go into custom packaging for a product to achieve retail success. Certainly retail packaging includes many different items, from folding cartons, corrugated boxes, metal tins, and plastic canisters to this novel one—a stand up pouch. This new kid on the block is part of the *flexible* packaging industry that includes plastic bags, paper bags, bubble wrap, foil bags, and more.

What goes into making a stand up pouch (also known as a stand up bag or retail stand bag) that makes it unique? First, it's made with multiple layers of scientifically engineered barrier film laminated together. This technique results in specific barrier properties to keep contents fresher for longer. These properties also keep out moisture, vapor, odor, and so on.

Manufacturers know every product needs to be protected in some way. In addition, some companies want their products to show through a window, while others design their packaging to be opaque because the contents may be vulnerable to UV rays or sunlight. Stand up packaging features that option, plus its film lamination process provides a second benefit: *it creates the strength and stability for the package to stand erect and stable on a store shelf.*

As a third benefit, because the product stands up on a retail shelf, the wide face, back, and bottom can display information about the product—what it contains and why it's good for you and so forth. The ability to print on this packaging allows for brand identification at the point of selection. That's key in grabbing a consumer's attention.

It shouts, "Pick me up and take me home!"

Who Are the Underdogs Now?

My company at StandUpPouches.net designs attractive stand up pouches *to stand up and stand out.* Since we began in 2005, we've been fortunate to land lots of "big fish" who love our packaging concept. But we actually cut our teeth—and built our business—on manufacturers with great products that must look amazing on the shelf to be taken seriously... the underdogs in the retail world.

Leaders in these companies knew their products had one shot at retail success. And while they felt confident in their products' merits (health benefits, taste, uniqueness, and combinations of these), their packaging also had to feature these merits. They knew consumers needed to get the full effect quickly, or they simply wouldn't buy. That's why packaging and success hang together in the retail world.

Early Challenges

In the early years, StandUpPouches.net faced challenges to stand out among its competitors in the packaging industry—an industry that's always been fragmented, even tired and stale. Typically, each packager would focus on the "big boys" and beat each other's brains out to get into these manufacturers. But they neglected the segment with the largest upside—the small- to medium-sized companies.

Our company realized if we went against the grain and showed up with something different from every other packaging company, we could attract more prospects and ultimately achieve more sales without requiring high-quantity production runs (50,000 pieces or more). Then we could adopt the strategy of taking a client from small quantities to large as they grew. In the long run, that would be worth more money and profit than trying to land "big boy" manufacturers at miniscule profit margins.

One of the first things we learned was this: *being different had to be our calling card.* Besides, we didn't have the staff or resources to send salespeople on the road knocking on doors to find clients who wanted and needed stand up pouches.

Around this time came the equalizer that enabled an underdog like us to compete with the big boys: the Internet. It had only been widely used by business for about five years, but it was the emergence of Google as the preeminent way to search for information that changed our business forever.

We noticed that the big boys continued to do things the way they always had—that is, send their salespeople to various companies, knock on doors, sell at the lowest possible price, rinse and repeat. However, companies were downsizing, and the buyers or decision makers didn't have time to meet with salespeople like they used to. Instead, they were turning to the Internet and specifically Google to search for what they wanted. Then (and only then) would they make a call or fill out a Contact Us form to reach a salesperson.

At StandUpPouches.net, we loved this! We didn't have the time or money to run around aimlessly anyhow. So we plowed our resources into creating content—*good, relevant content*—about our products and services. We wrote to suit Google. That way, when decision makers went looking, they'd most assuredly find us and then contact us.

Once prospects came to our site and started poking around, we had to be "Johnny on the Spot." That meant answering their questions and queries faster and more completely than anyone else. If we did this, we'd be in the driver's seat to close deals.

Ironically, this led to more leads and opportunities than ever before. Not necessarily more *business* yet, but more leads. We were one of the only companies specializing in stand up pouches on Google; no others came close to the quantity and quality of our articles and information. So finding leads wasn't a problem. But converting them to orders was.

Clients Wanted Printed, Not Plain, but We Couldn't Justify Large Print Runs

Those days, almost every company wanted printed, not plain, stand up pouches. But plain was all we could offer unless someone ordered 50,000 pieces. Plus, these buyers were already familiar with companies who sold stock stand up pouches in different sizes and colors (as we did). They'd simply put a label on them and try to sell them that way. Well, consumers could look at a stand up bag with an applied paper label (even a well-designed label) and compare it to an actual printed stand up pouch that only big companies could afford. No matter how good the product inside was, the unprinted stock pouch had little chance of standing out on the retail store shelf. It simply wouldn't be taken as seriously as a full-color printed pouch would be.

There was no shortage of small companies with money to spend and a desire to do what was competitively necessary. But they could *not* justify buying 50,000 printed stand up pouches (the minimum run quantity) when their orders from retailers only totaled 5,000 pieces. No one would buy ten times more than what they needed!

To be clear, these included innovative and great products; for example, a soy-based protein powder as a meal replacement for people wanting to lose weight without damaging their bodies; quinoa-based pilaf chock full of protein; incredible coated nuts with exotic flavors such as crème caramel, Italian black truffle almonds, or Herbs de Provence pecans.

Again, the products were awesome, but their packaging left a lot to be desired. If they made it to a store shelf, they would surely look inferior to the companies that had beautifully-printed packaging with vibrant colors and bold designs.

Bottom line: we had a boatload of opportunities but couldn't find a U.S. company that would run custom-printed stand up bags in reasonable quantities. So I did what any son of a butcher and a family of steelworkers would do: I called China!

CHAPTER 2:

CALLING CHINA

No one calls China out of the blue, of course. But through Internet searches, I tried to find overseas printing companies willing to quote on our projects.

It seemed the only way to find these companies was through a website called Alibaba—a searching service like Google but for Asian manufacturing companies. There I could find everything from balloons to carpeting to stand up pouches. But because the Chinese didn't spend the time or money to translate from Chinese to English, pricing and information were confusing. This made having any sense of trust and confidence slim to none. Still, I found plenty of companies that sold printed stand up pouches.

A small packaging company in Cleveland, Ohio, sending an RFQ (Request for Quote) to Chinese companies was like throwing a rock into the ocean. But I did it. I used their RFQ forms to send requests for printed stand up pouches. Weeks would go by before "Joe" or "Sally" (someone using an English-sounding name instead of their actual Chinese name) would reply and tell me the same thing I'd heard in the U.S.—only worse. Minimum run quantity: 100,000 (or more) for printed stand up pouches. Yikes!

My Only Shot

Given my overall strategy, I knew my only shot was to get a company to run smaller quantities. But how? I didn't speak Chinese, so how could I convey who we were and what we were trying to do? I looked for a translator, someone who spoke the language and could at least translate my RFQ. Then I could put in the "additional comments" section on RFQs something that explains my company so the Chinese manufacturer would understand.

Well, this didn't get the response I was looking for. But it did turn out to be the turning point in our business. Why? Because coincidentally the translator we hired had a brother-in-law or friend or some connection who had worked in Hong Kong as a vice president of Asian Sourcing for Kmart. (That was back in the days when Kmart was the retail giant, before Walmart ran over everyone in that category.) Our translator was gracious enough to say, "While I appreciate the hundred dollars you give me every time I translate a document for you, what you really need is someone in China."

Pivotal Resource

To say that meeting a certain gentleman from Michigan was a pivotal fork in the road would be an understatement. The then VP of Asian Sourcing for Kmart was Daryl Todd. Back in the glory days of Kmart and other retailers such as Sears and Montgomery Ward, Daryl was one of its key people in Asia. He had risen through the ranks as a store manager at various Kmart locations, then district manager, regional manager, and into the buying office. When given the opportunity to go to Hong Kong and coordinate overseas procurement, he jumped at it.

There, he would find suppliers and purchase products for Kmart stores around the world. Not only was Daryl responsible for the first dollar Kmart spent for items from beach towels to gas grills to car tires, but he traveled throughout China, Vietnam, Taiwan, Cambodia, India, and other countries to assure Kmart that these suppliers could provide what was ordered with consistent quality and on-time delivery.

Daryl developed such knowledge and skill evaluating companies and negotiating favorable terms for Kmart that he quietly became a trusted piece of its overseas operations. Unfortunately, in the United States, Kmart was "taking on water" trying to stave off this hot-shot giant retailer from Bentonville, Arkansas, Walmart. Despite having a multitude of stores and an established distribution network, Kmart was bleeding money. In early 2002, it had to file for Chapter 11 reorganization.

After nearly 31 years with Kmart, Daryl knew he'd need to reevaluate his career and make changes. He could return to the United States, but his passion and knowledge resided in Asia. He knew he could skillfully find suppliers, evaluate them, and create deals for companies wanting to buy overseas. Further, his greatest skill was finding and convincing suppliers, through his interpreters, to accept small- and medium-sized orders. He promoted the idea of starting a relationship that way and then building up to larger orders.

This is an important note: Chinese suppliers are no different than anyone else—they want large orders. But often they'd assume every order from North American companies would be massive, which wasn't always true. Certainly they were familiar with the large North American retailers such as Walmart, Home Depot, Target, and others, but these companies had started *somewhere.* They didn't initially order container-loads of product.

So after Kmart filed for bankruptcy, Daryl stayed overseas and started his own consulting and sourcing company doing what he does so well.

A Godsend

For us, Daryl Todd was a godsend. He took an interest in me and, without an order or even the potential of an order, he flew to Cleveland to meet with me. At that time, Daryl lived about nine months of the year in China and the rest in Florida. He and his wife had raised their daughters and son in China, and their children were now grown and on their own. So Daryl's wife, Michelle, found a home in Mt. Dora, Florida, where she could help their aging parents while he was building his sourcing business in China.

As we talked over lunch, Daryl made it perfectly clear that if I tried to "go it alone" in China, I would lose. "Now, Dave," he said in his Southern accent, "it may not happen on your first order or even the second, but it will happen. Somewhere along the line, a problem will occur. It could be quality, could be timing, could be lots of things. Then what are you going to do? Jump on a plane? Pick up the phone and call? But who would you call? Your main contact? Or where would you fly to? China is a big country. *What makes you think they'd pay attention to you?*"

Darryl's words were prophetic, as I later discovered. But suffice it to say, I knew I had found my connection in China. So we scheduled a time to travel to China together, and within a few months, my company was on its way.

My First Trip to China

The first time I traveled to China was a fact-finding mission. While locating suppliers for printed stand up pouches was definitely on my list, I had no idea what I would find, so I had to be prepared to switch gears if necessary.

At the time, I knew I needed to buy products overseas, but I just wasn't sure *which* products. Mostly, I was searching for factories that could give our company a competitive advantage—quality, price, or even designs that weren't available in the United States.

Specifically, I went to find suppliers of products such as these:

- Bulk bags used to transport bulk (3,000 pounds and up) products including sand, rock, chemicals, powders, etc.
- Woven polypropylene bags (reinforced shopping bags)
- Plastic corrugated boxes providing a returnable, more durable box (plastic that mimics paper)
- Low-melt plastic bags (used in industrial rubber making and compounding)
- Stand up pouches

To be honest, I wasn't counting on anything. My goal was to start relationships and learn how things worked. I traveled with Daryl and an interpreter named Joe Yu, who graciously set up appointments for us. We went into Chinese towns such as Shenzhen, Guangzhou, Qingdao, and Wenzhou touring factories. While there, I tried to impress on the people we met our desire to build our business and then they would build theirs, too.

Interestingly, Daryl had to pull me aside as he politely told me to "stop it." His comment burst my bubble and deflated my ego in the moment, but he continued, "Dave, the Chinese don't care about your plans, who you are, or anything you've done, period. All they care about are orders. Right now, they'll smile and nod and say nice things, but they don't care. You give them an order, *any order,* and then they will start to pay attention to you. Your job is to get back to the U.S. and send them orders."

As much as it was my way to paint a rosy picture for my new Chinese acquaintances, Darryl was right. I finally realized that whatever I said would go in one ear and out the other.

Meeting Candy

After about six days of meeting Chinese people and seeing their plants—while repeatedly hearing from Daryl to "tell them what I want and need, and if they can do something, they will cut to the chase by saying yes or no"—I found myself in Wenzhou, China. About two weeks before my trip, I was contacted via Alibaba by a lady named Candy in the flexible packaging business, specifically stand up pouches. Candy and I could communicate in English via email, but it seemed she had about a 70% grasp of the English language (better than most of the others I'd chatted with). I told her I was coming to China, but my time to visit factories was booked. Still, she insisted we meet. The only time for me was during a 30-minute span before checking into my hotel.

So there I was in the coffee shop of my hotel meeting with Candy on my own, no interpreter, no Daryl. I was exhausted from our travels. With Daryl's words echoing in my head, I overlooked the pleasantries and simply told Candy I didn't have much time. Then I explained the only way we could work together is if I could get very high-quality printed stand up pouches for very low minimum runs. That meant fewer than 5,000 pieces.

Every time I started to explain what our plans were, I'd stop myself and shut my mouth. Instead, I came right out and said,

"This is what I need; this is how we can work together. Give me an answer because I need to know now."

To my surprise Candy replied, "My uncle owns the factory. He believes in helping me start my own business as a woman here in China," which is something she felt proud about, "and I can persuade him to take your small orders." Immediately after she said this, I asked her a few more times to be sure I'd heard her correctly. Honestly, I wasn't expecting that reaction. Once I was convinced she could run high-quality printed stand up pouches with very low minimum runs, we shook hands and went our separate ways.

For the remainder of my first trip to China, I visited a few other factories, but I couldn't get Candy and her words out of my head. That was it, I thought. We could build an entire business around high-end printed stand up pouches. We'd go after small- to medium-sized companies and help them grow into large clients. We'd be a partner for them, helping them get onto store shelves at a competitive price and keeping them as clients for a long time.

By being able to run small quantities, we could change our message to everyone. We'd attract small companies and eventually large companies, too. They could try different flavors and versions of their products without having to commit to massive volume runs. Indeed, attracting *any* client large or small was more than we had before. Frankly, this approach would give us a chance to build more long-term relationships, which was our primary goal.

As imagined, we were enticed by the potential of working with large companies. But we fully focused our energy, time, and marketing messages toward companies wanting to compete against the big boys. They'd be the underdogs—the ones with great products but lousy packaging, no brand awareness, and a terrible shelf presence. We'd even target those that never had been packaged for retail sales before. To my knowledge, StandUpProducts.net was the only company focused on the small- to medium-sized clients at that time.

Since working with Candy (her real name is Chunjie Chen, and, at her request, I now call her Grace), we have produced close to 15 million bags and nearly $8 million in U.S. sales. Her factory continues to be our number one overseas supplier; however, we have since added two other factories in China as backups.

Open Doors

In subsequent trips to China, I traveled to Grace's plant, Zhejiang Deyi Soft Package Company LTD, to understand the equipment, printing capability, quality procedures, and so on. To my surprise, the workers have been extremely open and accommodating, allowing me to take photos and videos so I could clearly explain every step of the manufacturing process to our clients. This transparency opened up more doors and led to more orders. Why? Because we could explain printed stand up pouches not only via blog posts and eBooks, but also in how-to videos and other electronic formats. (More on our marketing strategy later.)

Don't Forget Team USA

By no means do we work solely with overseas suppliers; we have U.S. suppliers now as well. Being located in the United States has its advantages and disadvantages. For example, domestic factories are more expensive than our overseas plants by 20% to 30%. Unlike our overseas factories, they charge for every miscellaneous part of the printing process—from proofs to set-up fees to change orders. Printed stand up pouches can be made (and delivered) domestically in four to five weeks, compared with four to six weeks overseas and then another three to four weeks to ship them to the United States.

Domestic suppliers print flexographically. This isn't as bold and precise as the overseas factories, which print using the higher quality Rotogravure printing method. However, it still is very good.

When dealing with domestic factories, we strongly suggest you get a list of all miscellaneous fees and charges before you place your order so you are prepared. You don't want surprises. To be clear, domestic factories are not being tricky; they simply don't do a good job of explaining all parts of their process.

This does not mean we prefer one over the other; we give our clients the choice. If they feel a sense of patriotism by buying U.S.-made products, that's great. We like to support domestic businesses as well. But when a substantial cost difference is involved (and there is), we offer both options to our clients, and they choose.

I'd like to emphasize that we're part of a global economy. Was your cell phone or television manufactured in the United States? I doubt it. Many of our clients are being squeezed on multiple fronts: by retailers, by the rising cost of ingredients, by increasing fuel prices, and more. Any relief they can enjoy in their packaging costs is a welcome benefit.

CHAPTER 3:

TINY BUT MIGHTY EXAMPLES

This chapter features examples of three companies we have worked with. As case studies, they provide insight into our business model of helping companies replace inefficient, ineffective, and costly packaging with printed stand up pouches. Our pouches not only protect their products and keep them fresh, but they also build brands and tell the world why they're great.

Today, these clients have packaging that's as good as (if not better than) other examples in their industries. They can successfully compete with the "big boys" and win!

Let's explore how these three companies have made creative use of stand up packaging:

☐ Squirrel Brand

☐ Bob's Pickle Pops

☐ Garlic Clove Foods

Squirrel Brand

Since 1888, the Squirrel Brand Company has manufactured the ultimate nut. Born during the Industrial Revolution, Squirrel Brand has weathered two world wars, the Great Depression, and countless revolutions in the business world. Through it all, the company has remained steadfastly committed to producing the finest quality products for its customers.

The company was started in 1888 in Roxbury, Massachusetts, when the founder began selling mixed nut varieties from store to store via horse and wagon throughout Boston. Famously, Squirrel Brand nuts were carried to the South Pole by Admiral Richard Byrd on his first expedition to that region in 1929. They were also shipped all over the world during World War II.

When Squirrel Brand reached out to StandUpPouches.net, the nut company was in the midst of a push into the retail business. It had just started a new brand called Southern Style Nuts. With flavors and varieties such as Crème Brûlée Almonds and Fleur de Sel Pistachios, their packaging had to look as good as the products tasted. This meant not only that the film structure called for a design that protected the nuts and maintained their taste and freshness, but also that the artwork required many vivid colors. Our materials had to help make each color "pop."

Even more, Squirrel Brand needed our support to produce these custom-printed pouches quickly with a small order quantity and to be prepared to turn the machines on at a moment's notice if the brand sold quickly at the retailer. That's exactly what happened. At our overseas plant, we were able to run larger orders, hold them at our Ohio warehouse, and release them exactly when Squirrel Brand needed them to meet the demands of their retailers.

Squirrel Brand chose a premium film structure that included metalized polyester so the printing and colors had the WOW factor that converted to sales. Its major retail customer has since re-ordered several times. When they do, we release them from our inventory to replenish the supply seamlessly. That way, our client can fill its orders reliably. In the meantime, we restocked the inventory effortlessly in anticipation of their next run.

In our world, this is an example of Supply Chain 101—that is, our clients have what they need when they need it, and we replenish with every new order. Everyone wins!

Bob's Pickle Pops

It's hard to imagine pickle juice could have amazing health benefits, but that's exactly what it provides.

Bob's Pickle Pops are a vegetable-squeezed, frozen-juice ice pop treat with no added sugar and fewer than five calories. Children undergoing chemotherapy enjoy the salty taste, people with cystic fibrosis need lots of salt every day, and folks with MS enjoy the taste after their treatments. According to Carol S. Johnston, PhD, RD, in her article titled "Vinegar: Medicinal Uses and Anti-glycemic Effect" (http://www.bobspicklepops.com/health.htm), vinegar appears to be good for monitoring blood sugar levels. And having vinegar before a meal can blunt blood sugar spikes by 30 percent.

Many pickles are made with vinegars, which are known to boost the immune system, ease digestive disorders, and break down calcium deposits in a person's joints.

When Bob's Pickle Pops' marketing people approached us, they had wisely decided not to tout the health benefits of pickle juice by creating conservative packaging that looked designed by the *Harvard Business Review*. In fact, they did just the opposite. Their stand up pouches featured bold colors and a fun, quirky mascot appealing to women and men, young and old. At the same time, the packaging required strength and durability to protect the contents while standing erect on a store shelf.

The individual pickle pops that held the juice were already packaged. Our challenge? To make sure our stand up pouch would contain them, which isn't always easy.

Because liquid moves and flows, anytime a pouch was picked up, the liquid inside would shift back and forth. If the film design was cheap or flimsy, the pouch could fall down due the movement. At the retail level, a pouch that won't remain stable on a store shelf is destined for failure. So we provided the right film structure and are happy to say Bob's Pickle Pops continues to grow in popularity throughout the retail world. It has especially enjoyed success at Walmart.

We can't ever rely on a "cookie cutter" or "one material fits all" approach, so when designing the barrier film used for Bob's Pickle Pops, we had to evaluate where the product would be sold (Walmart initially) and how it would be merchandised (on a corner display). This meant possible rough handling due to rapidly filling into a display or being moved to other locations, and so on. Therefore, the material had to be resilient and strong, but flexible as well. If the film was too stiff or rigid, the bags wouldn't stand properly. Plus we knew consumers would freeze the entire package, so the material needed to be freezer safe, strong, and puncture resistant yet pliable. That way, if and when the pouch wasn't frozen or sat outside the freezer, it would still provide easy access into and out of the pouch.

Finally, the packaging has a large clear window area on the front of the pouch to allow consumers to see the individual pickle pops. This meant that whether the product was cold, at room temperature, or frozen, the film's clarity was critical and its quality had to be consistent. This is an example of the effort needed to truly understand not only how a product is packaged but also how it will be merchandised and viewed by the consumer.

Garlic Clove Foods

Garlic Clove Foods' mission is to "change the world" by creating convenient, easy-to-prepare side dishes that are healthy and delicious. Their pilafs are made with the perfect combination of 100% whole grains (quinoa, bulgur, and millet) along with vegetables, legumes, and natural herbs and spices. In fact, some benefits of its key ingredients often go unnoticed. For example, bulgur is a whole grain that feels and cooks like rice but is higher in protein, dietary fiber, and iron than rice. Quinoa, known as an "ancient" grain, is one of the few vegetarian sources of a complete protein. It contains all of the nine essential amino acids our bodies don't produce—ones we normally source from red meats, fish, poultry, cheese, and dairy. Finally, its dehydrated vegetables maintain more of their nutritional values than frozen or canned varieties.

These nutritional values are almost identical to fresh.

Garlic Clove Foods has become our classic client, one we built this company for and around. Amy and Dean D'Angelo pride themselves on being a family business that is committed to creating healthy food choices.

It started when they struggled with their child's food allergy. They had to make changes in their family's food choices but were shocked to find high sodium, preservatives, and other unhealthy ingredients in most products on the store shelves. As a result, they set out to create great-tasting yet healthy convenience foods.

Initially, they were building their business from the ground up, going to local farmers' markets in and around their Atlanta-area home. They didn't have the resources or the volume to order custom-printed stand up pouches. So, to protect their products, they chose one of our stock stand up bags, applied labels, and slowly built a following.

After a while, they decided to step out in faith and, with our graphic designer, created a printed stand up bag using subtle colors and a large clear window area accentuating the natural shades of the product itself. The film structure would protect the product from moisture and odor while maintaining the freshness and flavor.

Amy and Dean wanted the product itself to be the main focus, so the resulting graphic design and colors are restrained and soft. Even better, the main ingredients not only have a unique shape, they have color. A large window area is perfectly placed to be able to see the contents.

The film structure offered barrier properties to protect the contents from moisture while locking in the aroma of different spices. At the same time, it was stiff enough to consistently stand erect on a shelf. Plus, these packages can be layered strategically one on top of the other. This gives the product a distinctive artistic flair, regardless of where the pouches are merchandised—at a local farmer's market or a major retailer such as Whole Foods.

Today, Garlic Clove Foods products can be found in about 1,500 stores across the country, including Whole Foods Market and many independent natural food stores.

CHAPTER 4:

"PICK ME UP AND TAKE ME HOME"

A behavior shift was occurring right as we were embarking on building an online brand for stand up pouches.

Remember what was happening in 2008? The economy dove into the tank, the automotive industry was in the midst of the government bailout, and companies surviving the recession changed how they did business—specifically how they searched and ultimately purchased their packaging.

In my company's niche—stand up pouches in the flexible packaging industry—change ran rampant. Companies began to downsize; purchasing departments were being slashed and often eliminated. Only a select few people remained in charge of everything—not only manufacturing but procurement and even shipping and receiving. These people clearly didn't have time to meet with salespeople who knocked on their door, regardless of how great an offer they touted. Instead, purchasing agents turned to the Internet to find the products and services they needed.

As mentioned earlier, our company was an underdog. After we focused our business on printed stand up pouches in low quantities and connected with our overseas factory, we were open for orders. But much work still had to be done.

Fortunately, just as I had an "ah ha" moment about the potential for Internet marketing years before, I had another one when it came to marketing. It's called Content Marketing.

The Value of Content Marketing

Like many of our clients, we were small at that stage and didn't have the time, money, or resources to "pound the pavement." Plus our outbound marketing—cold calls, direct mail pieces, and even trade shows—produced little or no fruit. Given our overseas supplier connections, we knew we had a distinct advantage over other companies in our industry—that is, we could custom print stand up pouches with *quality* as good as anyone else in the industry. This allowed our clients to compete on the merits of their products and not lose out because their packaging wasn't as appealing as the products from the "big boy" companies.

However, we still had to locate companies that wanted what we offer: our printed pouches, designed to build their brands while protecting their products.

At that time, I was fortunate to attend a convention put on by the Content Marketing Institute. The folks staging it knew they had an identity problem; the term "content marketing" was new and unclear. According to the Content Marketing Institute:

"Content marketing is a marketing technique of creating and distributing relevant and valuable content to attract, acquire, and engage a clearly defined and understood target audience—with the objective of driving profitable customer action."

To me, this was code for pulling/pushing/leading clients to us instead of knocking on their doors.

Here's what has happened. If prospects are looking for our product and reaching out to us for guidance, the chances of engaging them and actually selling something is immensely greater than if we contact them to see if an opportunity or problem exists. This approach has played into our strengths. We have a great story to tell. We also have a unique opportunity for anyone looking to package their product and get it on a store shelf. And, frankly, we tend to be more cost effective than anyone in our industry.

Uncover Our Strengths

At this Content Marketing Institute convention, I became aware of dozens of ways to uncover our strengths and formulate them into marketing messages. I also learned just as many ways to deliver those messages without traditional (and expensive) outbound techniques such as cold calls, direct mail pieces, or even door-knocking.

To be specific, we discovered the value of the following:

- ☐ eBooks
- ☐ Videos
- ☐ White Papers
- ☐ Blogging
- ☐ Video Blogging (vlogging)

Further, we discovered delivery mechanisms that were

inexpensive yet used cutting-edge technology, such as:

- ☐ Hubspot (website platform)
- ☐ YouTube (video hosting)
- ☐ Wistia (video hosting for B2B)
- ☐ Compendium (blog posts)
- ☐ Brainshark (a service that plays like a video and has allowed me to embed my voice into PowerPoint presentations and then save and share it)
- ☐ PowToons (animation software that lets us create videos using stock cartoons and animated characters for graphics that are eye-catching and different)
- ☐ Animoto (software that played like a video and has allowed me to import various photographs and music to be shared)
- ☐ Postwire (software that allows me to group and combine multiple pieces of content, e.g., videos, eBooks, website links, etc., and then share everything in one main access point)

Then we promote and engage with our clients and prospects using popular social media tools such as:

- ☐ Twitter
- ☐ Facebook
- ☐ Instagram
- ☐ LinkedIn

Thinking Through the Elements of Content Marketing

Content Marketing isn't difficult, but it does take a lot of effort. It requires us to look at every single piece of our business and create eBooks, videos, white papers, and more. From answering a basic question such as "Do you sell printed stand up pouches?" to obscure ones such as "What size and color cartons do you use and what type of container will my pouches ship in?", we had to think through these and everything else in between—from film barrier properties and oxygen transmission rates to which Pantone colors we print.

Clearly, we had to think like our prospects from every stage of our business—from the initial fact-finding to marketing, to asking for the order and preparing them for a reorder later.

We also had to have the courage to be honest with them, which many in our industry are not. We explained that we're not a manufacturer; we are their representatives in the United States. And, yes, we have our own staff at the plant looking out for every one of our orders. They serve as our eyes and ears during the manufacturing process.

Client Engagement Is a Plus

Content marketing allowed us to engage with our clients, which has changed our business forever. I can't imagine ever working without it.

Ironically, and fortunately, the "big boys" in our industry have been slow to embrace content marketing. Sure, they have their websites, but they are behind in how they engage with their customers and potential customers, including discovering their interests and concerns.

This content marketing advantage has not gone unnoticed; we consider it a way to "level the playing field" and even out hustle our competition. I know for a fact we are gaining market share because of it. And we're determined to continue down this road.

Yes, they may have all the fancy equipment and incredible materials and films to choose from. But if the big boys can't find clients who need what they have—or get in front of them cost effectively to explain why they need it—we'll continue to beat them.

Many Tentacles Beyond Websites

When the Internet, Google, and searching online in general were new, the big conglomerates could pay top dollar to be found online. But so many tentacles go beyond simply being found on Google. They'll either have to pour a tremendous amount of time, money, energy, and resources into catching up or buy a company that's already Internet-marketing savvy.

My prediction: Those companies that position themselves online in ways the "big boys" need to emulate (and before they get there) have a great chance of either gaining market share or being acquired for a handsome premium—or both.

The days of buying online search results and credibility are over.

CHAPTER 5:

OUR SECRET WORKFORCE WEAPON

Let me introduce you to two key people in our company: Karen and Janelle.

For Karen and her husband Frank, it is a typical summer day. With the school year complete for Frank, a math teacher, they load up their Winnebago, their dog hops in, and they hit the road. Sometimes their RV "Big Baby" takes them to the great Smoky Mountains of Tennessee or down into Texas and Alabama, or maybe west to Yellowstone National Park.

Sure, they find plenty of time for sightseeing and enjoying nature, but instead of being "on vacation," Karen is an integral, fully functioning part of our company based in Cleveland, Ohio.

With Frank at the wheel of "Big Baby," Karen places a fresh mug of her favorite tea in a cup holder. She has already plotted the day's itinerary: Route 65 to 40 West and down Route 55 South toward Mississippi for a break. JoJo, their 11-year-old black lab and Doberman mix, has been fed and is taking his after-breakfast nap. But while most people would pick up a newspaper or Kindle to read the hours away, Karen has work to do.

Karen runs our company's entire stock pouch division.

She's responsible for all inventory, new stock pouch leads and orders, our warehouse staff, even our ecommerce folks who do the programming on our website. Singlehandedly, she oversees $500,000+ in sales, and that number is rapidly nearing $1,000,000.

Further, she is known as our First Response Coordinator, so she makes sure our customers have a WOW experience from the very beginning. That means Karen manages our "live" operators—those folks who answer inbound calls and leads. She also handles our outsourced WebGreeters, an overseas company that monitors our website for electronic leads. When I say "handle," I mean she teaches, trains, and monitors their responses to questions. Those queries could be about who should get a lead, who decides if the inquiry is a printed pouch opportunity or a waste of time, or any client issue that needs attention. I can honestly say that, without Karen, we wouldn't be where we are today; her influence has been *that* important.

I recall Karen commenting that she checks on existing orders, manages her staff, and even updates inventory while sitting at a traffic stop waiting for the light to turn green!

Then there's Janelle, who isn't waiting for a green light on the road as much as she's tending to her four boys (three small and one large one—her husband, Jimmy) in a completely different yet critical role for StandUpPouches.net.

Janelle's morning starts around 6 a.m. (often earlier) to the sound of a hungry newborn baby and a three-year-old and a five-year-old ready to start the day. She feeds the baby while scanning overnight emails from our factories in China, a world and 12 hours ahead of us, as she provides her bigger boys with milk and a morning snack. She juggles typing replies to our plant and updating clients on their orders while wiping milk off the baby. Then she moves on to review the day's "to-do list" with her husband before he takes a shower and heads off to his job.

After breakfast, Janelle goes back to scanning more emails and tending to her kids. If the baby cries or the boys fight, she simply steps away and takes care of things, then comes back once they've calmed down. Long and short, her entire day's activities revolve around the kids while her husband works from 10 a.m. to 8 p.m. On top of it all, Janelle is an aerobics instructor as well as the Saturday receptionist at her parents' hair salon.

Janelle is our production and shipping manager. That means every single custom order we run (about 70 percent of our business) crosses Janelle's computer. Once an order is placed, she starts tracking it. She looks for special instructions such as a Hot Rush or something needing a "color check" or even a sample made before authorizing an order for full production.

If anything isn't right, it's Janelle's job to alert the factory or members of our StandUpPouches.net team. Normally, she deals with 50 to 100 orders in different stages of "crisis." (I say "crisis" because every company has problems, some more critical than others.) Janelle has the unique ability to listen to the client, gather the necessary information, and then make things happen. Sometimes that involves asking the plant for favors to move up orders or even stop production. Other times that means getting a team member to call the client and discuss options.

For Janelle, her work life revolves around custom-printed stand up pouches and simplifying life for our North American customers.

Our Secret Weapon

If you didn't know I was referring to our company, you might assume I was describing a high tech firm with boatloads of cash, electronic options, and plenty of staff members to support those who handle critical functions in the organization. I chuckle every time someone thinks we are a "big" outfit atop the StandUpPouches.net tower in Cleveland, Ohio. (We're not.) In fact, I'm amazed that more companies, big or small, don't operate this way. And looking back on the last five years, it stuns me to realize I've hired all women and, in most cases, stay-at-home moms.

We didn't intend to develop our business around hiring women; it simply evolved that way. In fact, we now consider hiring competent women to be a "secret weapon" for us. I know this sounds biased, but I've seen this play out time and time again. Show me a mom who wants to work and give her the tools (computer, support, access to information/answers, etc.), and I'll show you someone who goes beyond "dedicated." She can juggle several things at once and transition from one job function to another without missing a beat.

As described earlier, a lot more goes into a printed stand up pouch than most people realize. These include different material structures, graphic design, color matching, production, shipping, inventory control, and project management as well as back office duties such as accounting and marketing. Every one of these responsibilities is handled well by women, mostly stay-at-home moms working virtually. As we've grown, we've added personal assistants for these ladies, so they manage a support staff as well.

What allows us to operate this way? How can we market our products and services, manage our staff, pull and push potential clients to our website, and interact with them at every step? It's because our process features a series of readily available tools that anyone can use. However, few companies choose to use them like we have.

Granted, without the high level of technology we've implemented (see next chapter), our business model simply wouldn't work. But it does! Employees work virtually from their own remote offices. Our 15 staff members range from graphic designers to project managers and bookkeepers and accountants. In addition, we have three staff members in mainland China who review and monitor all orders with our factories, ensuring they're done properly and on time.

However, we are all connected via Voice Over Internet Phone (VOIP), instant messaging, computers, and other tools. These not only make our company look bigger than it is; they help us respond faster with more current information. Regardless of where we are located, phone calls can be transferred, conference calls executed and joined, and computer monitors shared in an instant. Meanwhile, our clients feel like they're dealing with a sophisticated and seamless operation.

Further, when clients request a quote, most likely they have questions and need details. Questions might relate to how to create artwork, or how long it takes to make printed stand up pouches from start to finish, or what shipping options are offered. (See Chapter 9 for answers to these FAQs.) We not only anticipate these questions, but we also provide ready answers presented to our clients as part of our quote. This provides a WOW experience they remember. (See how we do this through our Postwire system, described in Chapter 6.)

Yes, we do have a traditional warehouse and carry inventory. Yes, we do have employees who pull and ship orders in our warehouses. But in the other parts of our business, we've had such success with our "virtual" way of doing things, we likely won't ever change back to a traditional model. This way is more effective and efficient *and* it reduces our costs. Most of all, our staff loves it!

CHAPTER 6:

MARKETING AND MANAGING—A BLUEPRINT

Several people have seen the success our company has enjoyed and asked for our help. For the record, I would have "killed" for someone to have provided specific help early in the life of our company. I've had to figure it out on my own—paying consultants well over one hundred thousand dollars and spending countless hours to see what works. Specifically, our Internet-marketing approach isn't difficult, but it takes consistently hard work, no shortcuts. Not long ago companies could "buy" their way to being found online by search engines, but the "big boys" such as Google and Bing have spent millions of dollars to eliminate these loopholes.

Here are various tools we use every day to accomplish these three critical things: Teach—Train—Get Found (TTGF).

- ☐ Video—YouTube
- ☐ Video—Brainshark
- ☐ Blogging—Compendium
- ☐ Website Platform/CRM—Hubspot
- ☐ Knowledge Base—Compendium

☐ Postwire—Secret Sauce (Teach/Train/WOW factor)

Let me explain how we use each of these at StandUpPouches.net.

Video

Our company uses two different types of video. One is pure video, using a video camera to produce a file that can be uploaded. Another type (and one just as important because of the type of information we're explaining) is a PowerPoint presentation uploaded (with voice embedded) to a video player. The PowerPoint option (using Brainshark software) works effectively because we can easily isolate certain pictures or features of a stand up pouch while I expound on it in the background. This allows me to go into great detail without having to memorize a script or be "on camera." Both styles have their place, and both can be found by search engines.

The Perfect Video

So many people get caught up in creating the "perfect" video—perfect lighting, scenery, scripting—and that's just nonsense. To be an effective teacher, the video has to have one key point with one key example, and then you're done.

If I'm attempting to teach someone about the right type of material to choose for a particular food product to be packaged in a stand up bag, the video must be informative but *not* promotional. If someone takes time to watch a video, the least we can do is provide something of value (e.g., how to save money, how to get the pouch done faster, how to protect their product more, etc.).

That's where many companies mess up. They make videos about how great they are instead of being transparent and specific about *teaching*. Our method goes against the grain, but it works because viewers trust us more. By giving information and *being helpful*, a bond forms. When the person viewing the video wants to proceed with the buying process, the chances of their choosing us increases because we told it the way it is. Not only do our video statistics show this (the number of video views + conversion rate into leads), but our clients tell us this directly.

Here's the bonus: because many of our videos are instructional and non-promotional, the same ones can be used to train/teach our staff. We don't hire people who have packaging experience, but we know quickly which people can learn fast. They can readily access our knowledge base of videos, our project managers, customer service, and shipping and receiving people, and so on.

For example, what better way to train new customer service representatives who wonder how we ship our products than to have them watch our own videos? Then they know what options we have and can provide those answers to our prospects. Even better, what if these customer service people verbally explained these options (having watched videos on the question/topic) and even forwarded the related videos directly to clients? That way, clients receive the information both verbally and visually.

I guarantee that our company looks more professional and bigger than we are because of our videos. As a result, our credibility with clients has increased dramatically over the years. Through our videos, we strive to answer every possible question pertaining to printed stand up pouches—from material selection and printing to colors, graphic design, and more. Each has been organized into a knowledge base related to certain keywords and subjects.

Note: The words "getting found" (GF) refer to being found online by Google and other search engines such as Bing and YouTube. (Yes, YouTube is a search engine that's often referred to as #2 behind big sister Google.)

Video Search Power

While creating a video to teach and train is important, missing an opportunity to use that same video to get found would be a huge mistake.

In the beginning, we put our videos on YouTube like everyone else. But frankly, we're a business-to-business type of company (B2B). Being lumped in with companies that produce funny, cute videos (Dollar Shave Club is an example) or show goofy college pranks on video can confuse our clients and prospects.

Thankfully, lots of B2B-friendly companies specializing in business videos are getting them found online. We use Wistia, which makes our videos extremely easy to upload and share. More than that, it's one of the few companies that understands search as it pertains to video.

Let me explain. To get a video "found," the video file itself needs be tagged and labeled and described in detail. That information is then given to Google and other search engines, indicating its location.

Let me repeat this important fact: If I've created a video about how to package protein powder using a printed stand up pouch, I first upload it to Wistia (or a service similar to Wistia). Then that video must be converted into a particular search-engine-friendly "code" that conveys to Google (and other search engines) what the video is about, where it's located on our website, what keywords are discussed on that video, why it is important, and so on. How many companies bother to do all this? Wistia has these tools built into its site using easy-to-understand buttons.

Without telling the search engines about your videos and the value they describe, you would be doing no better than throwing a rock into the ocean and hoping it gets found.

If you describe the video in detail the way Google wants it, the search engines will reward you, not necessarily with a good ranking, but they'll provide a little thumbnail next to the search results. That thumbnail denotes that a video pertains to that search.

Let's face it; people would rather watch a video than read a lot of text any day. So if a subject shows up as #10 on Google, but it's the only search result with a video associated with it, which listing do you think people will click on? They'll skip all of those above and click on the one with a video thumbnail.

Blogging

It wasn't that long ago that many thought blogging was a fad, a gimmick that gave everyone and anyone a voice if they used it. As far as printed stand up pouches are concerned, we use blogging to teach and train and get found (TTGF). Just as we've done with videos, we've created blog posts for every possible question we have received or anything someone might ask.

Blog posts pertain to the products that can be packaged in stand up bags, the industries that use them (retail, industrial, etc.), the features of stand up pouches (zip-locks, tear notches, gas-release valves, pour spouts, etc.), the materials—anything. Each post ranges from 400 to 800 words and includes a take-away value and most likely a video, too. This way, our prospects can learn about stand up pouches and decide if they want to pursue working with us. Indeed, we strive to keep all blog posts instructional, not promotional.

Like our videos, our posts are also used to train staff members, preparing them with the tools and answers they need regardless of their job position. Posts explain our process, our management team, our factory, our shipping and receiving options, and other parts of the business. Many answer questions clients might have, and it helps our internal staff as well.

Finally, these blog posts need to get found (GF). Yes, there's a science to this as well. They should be written so a person reading them can understand what's being said. At the same time, search engines have to be able to find them. This isn't easy because most companies try to accomplish both of these goals with their blog posts. However, Google and Bing, for example, have become adept at detecting "tricks" people try to influence them (such as using certain keywords over and over and over).

A good rule of thumb is to carefully think about specific people who will read a particular blog post, determine what's in it for them, and write it accordingly. Also, do research to determine what keywords to focus on and weave them solidly into each blog post a few times. Don't be too repetitive, though. If a human being can read your post and understand it, you have written it properly.

We use Compendium blogging software. It enables us to not only blog about certain topics and keywords but also to distribute those blogs to multiple channels at once, including Facebook, Google, and Twitter. Even better, through Compendium we can organize all of our content into a knowledge base that's easily found by both humans and search engines.

Producing a high volume of blog posts is great, but what's even more important? Having them organized effectively so as to convert readers into leads and sales. We've organized all of our blogs based on various topics and keywords so visitors can find what they're looking for quickly. Plus, the blogs show up as thumbnails, which makes it easier for them to be reviewed.

Website/Marketing Platform

Building our website onto the Hubspot platform was an easy choice for us, and is a platform that I highly recommend.

Over the years, we've had several iterations of our website, and that's all it was—a website. When I saw Hubspot, I was amazed at not only the simplicity of building and changing content on it but also at all of the other things it allowed us to do.

To be clear, Hubspot is a marketing platform, so having a website built on that platform is only one piece of the puzzle. Within Hubspot are sophisticated tools that allow us to research keywords pertaining to our business and, even better, to see which keywords our competitors were being found with for our own search engine optimization (SEO).

Within Hubspot is a customer relationship manager (CRM) where our leads can be stored and divided into subcategories. We can target potential clients interested in stand up pouches for food with our unique information. Then we do the same for potential clients interested in packaging non-food items, and so on. With simple instructions, Hubspot can be told to automatically send certain types of content over a certain period using auto-responders and by parsing responses into different groups. With simple clicks of a button, customized website landing pages can be created, videos can be uploaded, and content can be shared over multiple social media channels, such as Facebook, Twitter, and Pinterest.

Yes, Hubspot has changed our business. Why? Because everything is seamlessly integrated and can be updated to generate more traffic to our website. That brings in more leads and ultimately more sales. Hubspot features many more tools we can use in the future, and we'll implement them, too.

StandUpPouches.net would certainly not be as successful today without this marketing platform.

Knowledge Base and Compendium Blogging Software

Let me elaborate on the knowledge base component as I discuss our blogging strategy, which utilizes Compendium.

If all of the content we've created (and will continue to create) isn't organized for clients and staff to use, we will miss out on a tremendously huge opportunity. Our knowledge base provides us a means to teach, train, and attract new clients. That's why we've invested in Compendium blogging software.

With Compendium, every blog post we've written and every video we've uploaded can be organized, tagged, and subsequently searched using particular keywords. For example, if potential clients want to learn about packaging dry food products, they can find and then view countless posts on that topic. If staff members have a question about printing certain colors or equipment restrictions, they can enter certain keywords and be taken to specific blog posts and videos. Clearly, Compendium gives us an excellent way to organize and share our content for both marketing and instruction.

Postwire

Because printed stand up pouches require a consultative selling strategy with no "one size fits all" approach, every client has different questions at different times throughout the sales process.

I have emphasized the role that content plays to Teach, Train, and Get Found (TTGF). Just as we've collected blog posts into a searchable knowledge base using Compendium, we also offer a better system for organizing everything else. It's called Postwire. Its tagline is: The Personal Sharing Tool for Sales People and Their Buyer.

These illustrations show one of the many Postwire pages we have created for our staff pertaining to printed stand up pouches. One thumbnail features several printing specific (PS) pieces of content our staff can share with a prospect or use to answer a client's question. Another thumbnail shows pieces of content pertaining to cost savings (CS) so we can enlighten a prospect with ways to save money. These thumbnails open to another group of content, which could be anything from a link for a blog post to a video or even a Word document or PDF attachment.

Here's the thought process behind this system: By providing an abundance of information organized according to what they're interested in (*organized* being the operative word), our clients come away assured they have found the right supplier (and that would be us). And they'll see how complex a printed stand up pouch can be. Now, we don't want to intimidate our prospects, but it's important they know how much is involved—more than just slapping something onto a piece of plastic. Having our content organized and presented in such a clear, complete way leaves a lasting positive impression on our clients.

Further, one of our goals is to WOW our clients—not only when they come to us initially but throughout the sales funnel. While many companies concentrate on "getting an order," that's only part of the process. If we can WOW clients from the time they come to our website until their product is delivered, we have a great chance of creating a happy customer and setting ourselves up for repeat business.

A Postwire page for one of our customers will include the project manager's info, the approved artwork, and even details about the order. We even use Postwire to communicate with our clients after they have placed their orders.

Opening these thumbnails leads to other pieces of info so the client can feel "warm and fuzzy" about the order being in good hands. This creates the WOW effect we want.

Naturally, once their orders are placed, clients have different fears and concerns (e.g., when will it be done, how will it ship, who should they contact if they have a change or problem, etc.). We proactively provide this information well ahead of time so they have it if and when they need it. As a bonus, our staff avoids fielding unnecessary questions.

It's important to note our willingness to being available via traditional means, such as phone calls, emails, and virtual meetings. But with Postwire, we give information clients can consume anytime they need it or if something comes up. Our clients *love* this proactive approach, and we do, too.

As a result, StandUpPouches.net comes across as a bigger company than it is. Compare that to most other companies sending a regular email with, say, seven attachments. That not only looks awkward, but also rarely do the attachments get opened.

The stand-up pouch business in North America is a $6 billion (with a B) industry and is still growing. We aim to become the #1 online brand for printed stand up pouches in North America by creating a WOW experience for our clients. That has to happen from the time they first contact us until long after their custom stand up bags have delivered. And while we love technology, we won't hide behind it. Rather, we're driven by our old-fashioned values of wanting to help our clients stand out in their markets!

CHAPTER 7:

ENVIRONMENTAL INFORMATION FOR PACKAGING

Are stand up pouches environmentally friendly? The answer in one word is yes. Here's why we can say that.

Stand up pouches are made from multiple layers of scientifically engineered barrier film laminated together. This lamination is key. Why? Because the laminated film provides strength and stiffness so the pouch can stand effectively. It can also withstand puncture and rough handling. Further, the laminated film provides crucial barrier properties that protect the contents from moisture, vapor, odor, UV rays, and other negative elements.

Traditional bags such as sandwich bags, produce bags, or grocery store bags are made from a single layer of film, also called a mono layer. Bags made from this type of film don't have nearly the strength or barrier properties as bags made from laminated film. In fact, other than the thickness, most people can't tell the difference between monolayer film and laminated film. As a result, most (if not all) landfills and recycling programs group all plastic bags into massive *bales* of plastic bags. These bales get chopped and ground into tiny pieces called regrind; they become main ingredients in plastic products such as plastic toys, picnic tables, plastic lumber, garbage cans, etc. Landfill-friendly stand up pouches can be thrown away as trash. (NOTE: Its recycle code is likely an R7.)

Because stand up pouches are made from laminated film (not the mono or single-layer film), they aren't biodegradable. However, here's where many people get confused. For anything to be biodegradable, it needs to be exposed to air and sunlight over time. However, these two elements weaken the packaging and allow it to "break down."

Today, throwaways go to a landfill as trash or garbage. Let's face it, trash stinks. So the fastest way to neutralize the odor of garbage is to bury it deep into the ground and then cover it. Once it's covered, then it's no longer exposed to air and sunlight; therefore, nothing will break down—not paper boxes no paper bags nor stand up pouches.

To be clear, we are all for helping our environment. While there have been advancements in fancy (expensive) new barrier films that show great promise to protect and keep products fresh, the industry just isn't there yet. Either the pricing is exorbitant, the results aren't good enough yet, or both.

However, applying the 3 R practice (reduce, reuse, recycle) is still highly appropriate. Studies have shown that, far and away, the best way to help our environment is not with fancy new films or expensive additives or incinerators that burn trash and turn it into fuel. Rather, the solution lies in *reducing* how much plastic and packaging is used. It's in this category that stand up pouches shine. They can replace bottles, glass jars, plastic pails, and even cans that share the same negative attributes: they're heavy, take up a lot of room to store, use a lot of fuel to ship, and require a lot of energy to make.

Considering these alternatives, stand up pouches are indeed excellent for the environment.

CHAPTER 8:

FOUR STYLES OF STAND UP POUCHES

When constructing a stand up pouch, a main differences in design is in the style of the bottom gusset. Four main styles are described here, as well as additional styles for packaging liquids.

Round:

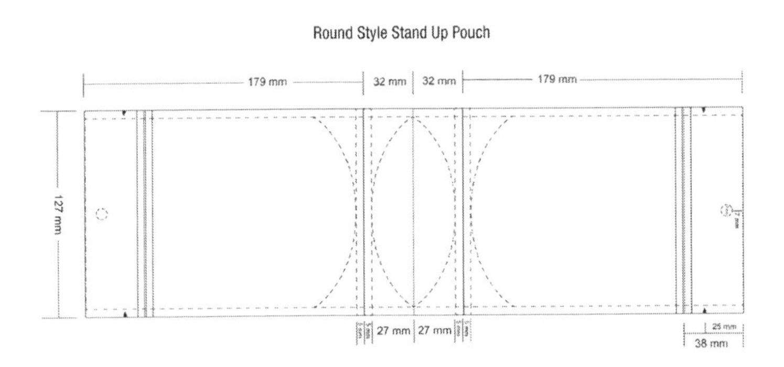

The round-bottom gusset, often referred to as a Doyen style, tends to be the most prevalent today. Here, the film is joined at the bottom of the stand up bag, which creates a half circle (or smiley face), while the front and back panels sealed to the bottom gusset provide rigidity and strength. This style relies on the strength of the film and the seals. It works well for products that weigh less than one pound (e.g., spices, Stevia, croutons, etc.).

K Style:

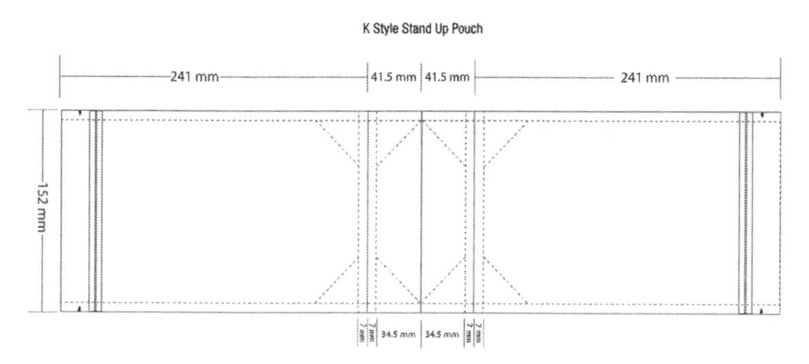

Like the round style, the K style refers to what the bottom gusset looks like after it's sealed. Here, the corners are sealed as well as the bottom, which creates a shape like the letter "K." The film and the seals provide much of the strength.

A K-style bottom gusset works well for products that weigh more than one pound. They're generally used for up to two-and-a-half pounds and even up to five pounds. This style is appropriate for rice, beans, granola, and cereal, as well as for non-food items such as chemicals and powdered soap.

Plow:

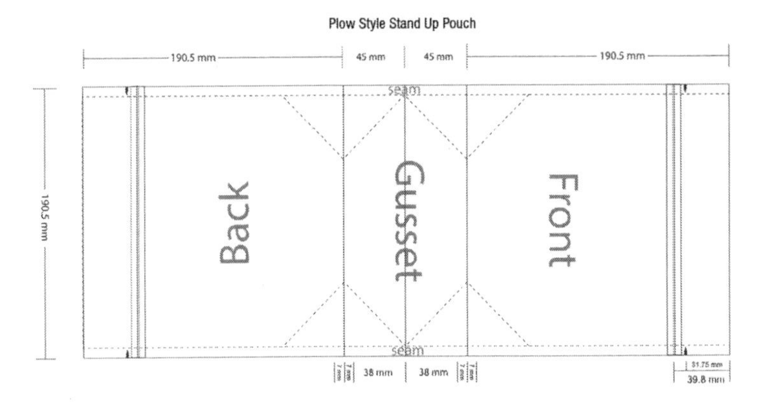

On a plow bottom, the corners of the pouch are sealed (like the K style), but by design the weight of the product itself pushes or "plows" to the bottom of the pouch. In reality, it's the product that creates the strength of the bottom gusset, while with the round and K styles, the sealing of the film creates the strength.

A plow-bottom gusset is used for dense, heavy products such as rock salt, sugar, heavy beans, chemicals, etc. Products weighing more than five pounds use a plow-bottom style.

Flat Bottom–Side Gusset:

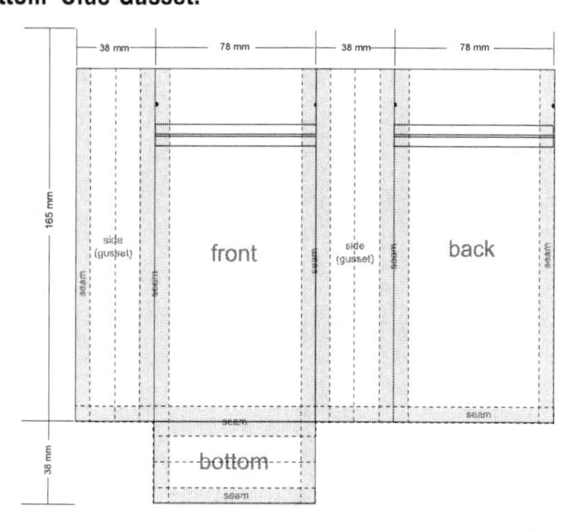

This style—the newest in the flexible packaging industry—was not created to hold a certain amount of weight. Rather, it's meant to mimic a folding carton, otherwise known as a cereal box style. Pouches made with a flat bottom and side gussets work very well with products weighing more than one pound. Because of its unique shape, this style holds much more than other stand up pouches with more traditional bottom gussets. It also uses up to 15% less film than the other styles.

To summarize, here are guidelines to go by: Use a round-bottom gusset if your product is less than one pound.

- ☐ Use a K style if it's more than one pound and up to two-and-a-half pounds.
- ☐ Use a plow-bottom gusset for two-and-a-half pounds and more.
- ☐ Consider using flat-bottom stand up pouches for products exceeding one pound in weight and if you are interested in replacing folding cartons and corrugated boxes.

Printed Stand Up Pouches for Packaging Liquids

Packaging liquid in a printed stand up pouch continues to grow in popularity around the globe. It reflects the increasing number of retailers and consumers who want to get rid of the rigid plastic and glass packaging that cost more (in terms of price as well as the energy required to produce them).

With the advancement in the barrier film layers, stand up pouches with spouts can be used to hold everything from fruit juice and water to soap and even oil and alcohol. This was nearly impossible in the past because these items were "aggressive" on certain films. However, that is changing.

What should you know when packaging liquid in a spouted stand up pouch? Ask these three questions:

1. How do you plan to fill these pouches? A spouted stand up pouch can be filled directly through the spout and cap or through a void or open area on the top of the pouch that will need to be sealed once the pouch is filled. In this situation, the stand up pouch will arrive with the spout and cap already affixed to the bag. This void will be the only area available for filling.

2. Do you want the spout and cap in the center or on one of the sides (can't have both)?

3. Do you even need a spout and cap? We provide many liquid pouches without a spout and cap (which adds cost). Instead, they have a tear-off or cut-off area that's used for the liquid to be poured out. This style works for single-serve (one time use) pouches.

NOTE: Spouted stand up pouches can have round, K-style, and/or plow-bottom gussets. The flat-bottom style has not performed well with liquids, so it's not recommended yet. As always, trust your packaging professional for guidance and direction.

CHAPTER 9:

ANSWERS TO KEY PACKAGING QUESTIONS

It isn't the person with the best idea who wins. Rather, it's the person who has the greatest understanding of what matters most to people.

We strive to understand the personalities, fears, and worries of our small clients (including startup companies) as much as those concerns for our mid-market and larger clients. But we also know they're radically different.

Stand up pouches are used from the smallest of companies all the way up to massive corporations, including Nestlé and Procter & Gamble. In our company's history, we've had immense success with small companies (those with 1 to 100 employees) and mid-market companies (between 100 and 500 employees). Yet a completely different dynamic exists between the small and the mid-market. There are different fears and worries as well as different frequently asked questions (FAQs).

Let's examine both groups in further detail.

We've identified organizations between 1 and 100 employees as being in the category of "small." However, we've found the average number of employees who work at small companies to be fewer than 20. Often, the owners are recent retirees who are pursuing their dreams of owning a company to bake a granola recipe or produce a pet treat. Or it's a husband and wife who take their savings and attempt to create a new income stream for one or both of them. Some of our clients have been downsized out of a corporation and are using their severance packages to chart different careers. Some are even recent college grads with fire-in-the-belly entrepreneurial spirits who want to work for themselves instead of being on someone else's payroll.

Regardless, those in the segment we call "small" have incredible drive and work ethic. They'll labor all hours of the day and night to develop and ultimately sell their products.

We've discovered that these folks will either (1) completely ignore packaging until the last second, at which point they realize their products need to ship in a week; or (2) they assume all packaging is the same and it doesn't really matter. Many have no idea what type of packaging they'll need to protect their product and/or tell their story and build their brand.

Quite a science exists for developing laminated film combinations for particular products. There is no such thing as one film combination that works for all products. Therefore, we need to know answers to these questions and more:

- ☐ What is being packaged?
- ☐ How heavy is it?
- ☐ Is it light, fluffy, or sharp/pointy?
- ☐ How will it be filled, stored, shipped?
- ☐ Where will it be sold?
- ☐ Will it be hot or cold or frozen?

Knowing all of these factors is critical for us to provide the right film structure at the right price point. Caution: Too many film layers with the wrong films could mean paying too much. The other extreme would be to have too little protection, allowing the product to go bad or stale, or the bag won't stand properly.

Using stand up pouches that are custom printed adds another layer of complexity. Products need the right film layers for protection. As well, one of those layers will be the printed layer, so now graphic design and colors and printing cylinders have to be taken into consideration.

Five Most Frequently Asked Questions by a Small Client

1. How much do stand up pouches cost?
2. How do I create my artwork?
3. What if something goes wrong?
4. How long does it take?
5. What material should I use for my product?

How much do printed stand up pouches cost?

As anyone can imagine, this depends. It depends on the size of the pouch, the materials used for the laminate layers, the complexity of the printing, and the features on the pouch itself (a zip-lock, tear notch, pour spout, hang hole, etc.). Here, let's examine basic printed stand up pouches in a couple of sizes and materials with a zip-lock and tear notch and even a hang hole (premium features like a gas-release valve and a pour spout are additional charges and not part of this review).

Keep in mind that these are ranges. The final price depends on the type of material chosen (clear, metalized film, aluminum foil, or combinations of these), the thickness of material, the complexity of printing (i.e., number of colors, how much print coverage on the bag), and the type of additional features you want (zip-lock, tear notch, hang hole, etc.).

We provide pricing based on simple quantity breaks: 10,000; 25,000; and 50,000 pieces.

4 x 6.5 x 2.5 Stand Up Pouch

10,000 pieces approximate cost between
$.15 cents and $.18 cents

25,000 pieces approximate cost between
$.12 cents and $.17 cents

50,000 pieces approximate cost between
$.08 cents and $.15 cents

5 x 8 x 3 Stand Up Pouch

10,000 pieces approximate cost between
$.16 cents and $.195 cents

25,000 pieces approximate cost between
$.13 cents and $.18 cents

50,000 pieces approximate cost between
$.10 cents and $.16 cents

6 x 9.5 x 3.25 Stand Up Pouch

10,000 pieces approximate cost between
$.17 cents and $.21 cents

25,000 pieces approximate cost between
$.14 cents and $.20 cents

50,000 pieces approximate cost between
$.11 cents and $.17 cents

7 x 11 x 3.5 Stand Up Pouch

10,000 pieces approximate cost between
$.18 cents and $.22 cents

25,000 pieces approximate cost between
$.15 cents and $.21 cents

50,000 pieces approximate cost between
$.12 cents and $.18 cents

NOTE: These are meant to be estimates and ranges. Further, they do not include printing cylinders/plates or freight.

Printing cylinders/plates from our overseas factory are in the $225 to $350 range (you need one per color, and these are one-time charges). Printing cylinders/plates from our U.S. factory are in the $350 to $450 each range.

How do I create my artwork?

Some clients have an idea of what we mean by artwork, while others don't have a clue, and yet others fall somewhere in between. Regardless, creating the right artwork for the product is one of the key problem areas for printed stand up pouches.

Printing on stand up pouches is unlike other types of printing. First, the printing goes on flexible film, not paper or a brochure or even a cardboard box. Thus, for someone who is familiar with printing on a business or greeting card, colors will look different than expected when printed on a clear film, an opaque one (metalized film), or aluminum foil.

Indeed, the entire process of printing stand up pouches is different. When the ink is placed on top of what's being printed (e.g., a box or card), it's called surface printing. With printed stand up pouches, it's referred to as trapped printing. This means the printing is done on one of the film layers and then that film layer is trapped and laminated to other layers—at least one above and one below it. That way, the printing cannot be scratched or marred. In addition, when these layers are added above and below the printed layer, this can affect the final color.

A recommendation that's most critical to your success is this: *Use an experienced graphic designer to create your artwork.* Don't go it alone. Even more important, use a graphic designer who has experience with printed stand up pouches or any type of flexible packaging. And choose a pro who isn't afraid to say, "I'm not a hundred percent sure about a certain detail. Let me ask what's the best thing to do in this case."

I'd like to expand on this point because it's happened so many times and with so many colleagues in our industry that it's gone beyond a phenomenon.

Remember, as noted, printing on stand up pouches is not the same as printing on a brochure or other type of product. As a result, we've had run-ins with graphic designers (often freelance) who feel so desperate to please (and keep) their paying clients that they claim they can create graphics for a printed stand up pouch. They mistakenly assume it requires the same process as designing a logo or letterhead or retail sign. Also, they're used to having 23 different colors to work with, while a printed stand up pouch can use only 10 to 12 colors.

What happens? Instead of saying, "I need help" to understand our specifications, they often blame us—the printed stand up pouch company. In fact, it seems all business owners know a graphic designer (a relative, a friend, a spouse, or significant other) and assume they'll get a discounted price. In reality, the design task ends up becoming far beyond what the client expected or could afford to pay. Some have even walked away from doing a printed stand up pouch (and in drastic cases walked away from their business) when they couldn't get it at the price point they needed. Unfortunately, their inexperienced designers had produced graphics that went beyond what could be printed cost-effectively. It's incredibly frustrating to set up a battle when their livelihoods are at stake.

Whether you're a client looking for printed stand up packaging or a graphic designer selected to create the package's design, the solution is to *communicate*. Naturally, we want all parties to get what they want. So if the graphic designer communicates with us what the client wants and needs, we can in turn work to accommodate everyone. *The goal is to minimize the time and expense the graphic design process takes.*

Yes, graphic designers should be able to take your thoughts, goals, and dreams of how you (not them, but *you*) want your printed packaging to look. Make sure the designer you hire is well versed in all the graphic tools needed and is willing to communicate!

NOTE: To be clear, we love graphic designers. We have three on staff, each serving in different roles. One is able to make sure graphics a client has had designed are "print ready" (at no extra charge); another creates a client's artwork from scratch; yet another does both.

Our Artwork Guidelines (ABC Packaging Direct and StandUpPouches.net)

We print edge to edge, so if you have a 6 x 9.5 x 3.25 stand up pouch, your available space (or real estate) is 6 inches x 9.5 inches on the front or face of the stand up pouch and 6 inches x 9.5 inches on the back. The bottom gusset can be printed, but not always registered print (like a bar code). (Always check with your packaging professional for guidance.) To be sure, keep the bottom gusset a solid color or clear. If you want to explore printing on the bottom gusset, check with your packaging professional.

Finally, make sure you have a 2mm border on the left and right margins of your pouch (front and back) of a consistent color. We run these on high-speed lines and the pouch film will want to "drift." Be aware that matching up a print to the very edge is impossible for anyone. Having the 2mm (which is a very small area) will give us enough room to make sure your printing looks awesome every time. (This is a trick we've learned over 25+ years.)

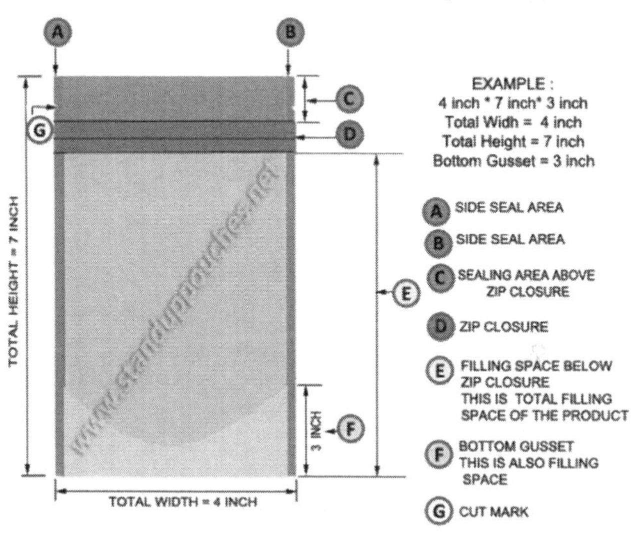

What if something goes wrong?

Our job is to take a client's artwork and marry it to the right film structure to protect the product and keep it fresh. At the same time, we have to print the colors in the artwork with the desired "pop" and vibrancy the client intends. But achieving all this is easier said than done.

In printed flexible packaging jargon, the word "something" in the phrase "What if something goes wrong?" almost always refers to the actual printing on the stand up pouch. If a flexible package wasn't made properly (e.g., a seal was bad or a zip-lock wasn't applied properly), people understand it will be corrected. However, many small business owners don't have the confidence or knowledge in the area of printing and color matching to understand their options. They simply don't know what to expect.

Briefly, here's our process. After a client submits artwork, we make an electronic proof, usually a jpeg or pdf type of file. First, that proof shows an outline of the stand up pouch with the particular size of the bag along with all the graphics placed on that outline where the client wants them. This outline indicates the size (outside length and width and bottom gusset as well as inside dimensions).

Second, the electronic proof shows features such as a tear notch or hang hole or zip-lock, showing where on the pouch they'll appear.

Third, the proof lists all of the colors to be printed on the stand up pouches.

Then the critical communication begins between the client's graphic designer and our designers. Once the artwork is ready, it's our job to figure out how to print it on flexible film. In most cases, we can print up to 10 colors, with our new press printing up to 12 colors. Based on the detail, complexity, and quantity needed, we decide which printing machine to run it on. We also take into consideration the kind of product being packaged and the type of film the client selects.

For example, let's say a client is packaging cereal and wants a printed stand up pouch with a clear window or clear area on the bag so the product can be seen. We take that into consideration. Conversely, if a client doesn't want a viewable area, an opaque film will be used. Just as a painter can paint certain colors on certain materials (canvas, paper, glass, etc.), the same is true for printing flexible packaging. Therefore, colors will look different when printed on different types of materials (clear film versus opaque film).

After we make an electronic proof (knowing it's a starting point and everyone's computer monitor is set to different levels) and the client places an order, we'll create printing cylinders. These are made from etched or engraved metal. Each color of a client's artwork requires one printing cylinder. If the artwork calls for eight colors, then eight printing cylinders are needed. Once the cylinders are made, they're coated with ink, and a sample of the printing is created. To be clear, this is not a sample of the pouch itself; rather, it's a sample of the *printing,* called a film proof. This film proof is on a very thin structure and is meant to depict what the actual printed colors will look like on the film.

Our client will either see a picture of this film proof or request the film itself. However, this film proof is made with a small, unsophisticated printing press, not what we would use in final production. So the colors won't be exact and the printing registration won't be perfect. However, this proof still gives the client an excellent starting point and reference.

From there, knowing that this film proof is a thin film and the final pouch will have other layers laminated to it, we bring out similar-looking production pouches. Specifically, we show how we overlay and "sandwich" other film layers above and below the printed layer. This provides the client with an as close-to-final look as possible.

Over the years, we've printed millions of pouches and retained samples specifically so clients can see what certain colors will look like on a finished pouch. As noted, colors printed on clear film look different than if the same color is printed on an opaque film such as metalized or foil material. Again, that has to be taken into consideration.

This is one way we go into detail about what the printed pouches will look like, as part of our service. We do this ahead of final production so clients can be highly aware of how certain colors will look and react on printed film. Not only do we communicate this with our clients, we also do the same with the printers in our company. That way, they are well aware of the colors and final result the client is looking for *before* a job is run. Then if something goes wrong that pertains to the printing, we reference all the samples and information we provided the client *and* the printers.

We aim to do everything we can to manage expectations both for the client and for the printers in our company. The final result will *never* embarrass a client, meaning a color meant to be red won't get printed green or yellow or something else. However, if we run a certain color that isn't quite right, after taking detailed notes, we'll continue to adjust it on subsequent runs to achieve the exact color. Because the printing and ink used are controlled by sophisticated computers monitoring the exact percentages of colors, if something needs to be adjusted, analyzed, or tweaked, it can be done quickly and efficiently.

How long does it take to make printed stand up pouches?

Answering this question comes with this caveat: the artwork and graphic design have been completed and accepted by the client. At that point, the clock starts ticking.

Printed stand up pouches are made from multiple layers of film laminated together. Each layer serves a specific purpose, whether it's strength or durability, barrier protection, odor or moisture resistance, and of course the printing itself.

The first five days for a printed stand up pouch involve making printing cylinders. Here, the artwork is etched into steel and then formed into cylinders that will be mounted onto the printing press. Each color of the artwork requires its own cylinder. The printing cylinders are used for creating only the printed layer; the other layers to be used are not printed and are made separately.

Once the printing cylinders are complete, the printed layer of the stand up pouch will be finished. This printed layer is a thin substrate that, by itself, has little strength or durability. Each color is applied at individual bays or sections of the printing machine. Then this printed layer is set aside, awaiting the completion of the other layers that will be used to form the finished printed pouch.

As mentioned earlier, the other layers of a printed stand up pouch all serve different purposes. One layer determines if the pouch will be clear (or have a window so the product inside can be seen) or will be opaque to prevent light from entering or to keep the product from being seen. All the film layers are then laminated together, with the printed layer being one of the middle layers. It's actually sandwiched between films so the printing can't get scratched or marred.

Now that the layers are all joined together, they are wound into master rolls that are then sent into an oven (approximately 140 degrees F depending on the structure and the thickness of the structure) for up to 48 hours to "cure." This curing is essential to ensuring the films are bonded and won't separate. After the curing process, the film is then unwound and converted into the intended size. That's when the features (zip-lock, hang hole, gas valve, pour spout, etc.) are added.

Generally, printed stand up pouches take 4–6 weeks to produce after the artwork is finalized. Here is a normal schedule at a glance:

- □ Week 1: Printing cylinders are made.
- □ Weeks 2 and 3: Printed film layer and other layers are made; the film is laminated.
- □ Weeks 4 and 5: Film is converted into finished pouches.
- □ Weeks 6 through 9: Shipping/transportation/ delivery to your door

Note: If printing cylinders are already in place, then the lead time for repeat orders is usually 18 days plus shipping.

What material should I use for my product?

When considering which material to choose for printed stand up pouches, step one is asking questions so you clearly understand what you are packaging. Step two explores the type of structure needed based on your criteria for the particular printed stand up pouch or stand up bag. This involves how much weight will be put into the pouch, the conditions the stand up pouch will be subjected to, the ultimate use for the stand up bag, and even who the end user will be.

The information below sheds light on the advantages and disadvantages of the different barrier film structures available.

NOTE: Your Criteria™ determines the thickness of your pouch. Your Criteria™ + the thickness + the quantity needed = the price per pouch.

Clear Structures and Metalized Film Structures: These are usually close in price when everything else is equal (depending on your criteria). Both can be made with excellent barrier properties, strength, and durability, too.

Aluminum Foil Structures: These tend to be more expensive than clear and metalized structures, as they generally have superior barrier properties over clear and metalized film. Remember, aluminum foil is just one layer of the overall structure. It all depends on your criteria.

Boilable Structures: These can be made from clear film, metalized film, and foil structures. As mentioned, clear and metalized films tend to be close in price point, whereas aluminum foil tends to be more expensive. Again, it depends on your criteria.

Microwaveable Structures: These are made from clear films that are laminated to provide barrier properties and the strength to withstand microwave heating elements. Anything metalized wouldn't work in a microwave. The price points for microwaveable clear films are in line with other clear films and are based on your criteria.

YOUR CRITERIA™

a) What you are packaging (is it a powder, a paste, a liquid; is it sharp, heavy, oily, greasy, etc.)?

b) Do you want to be able to see your product or have a clear window on your pouch?

c) How much weight you are packaging into the pouch (150 grams, 1 pound, 5 pounds, etc.)?

d) What style pouch do you want (will it be a stand up pouch and need to stand, or will it be a flat pouch that hangs in a display, or a gusseted pouch, or a tamper-evident pouch that loads from the bottom, etc.)?

e) What features do you want (zip-lock, tear notch, hang hole, liquid pour spout, etc.)?

f) What kind of conditions will the pouch be subjected to (will it be in a chemical factory and thrown off of a pallet; will it be used by a consumer who will open it and place it back into his/her pantry; will it be used in a dirty, greasy industrial plant, or will it be used in a clean-room electronic facility, etc.)?

g) What price point do you want/need to be at? Do you want the cheapest possible price so your packaging keeps your product fresh for 30 days, or do you want something that will keep your product fresh for 12 months (plus can withstand high temperatures, a 15-foot fall, etc.)?

NOTE: Concerning cost, all of these factors noted play a role in the film structure and ultimately the thickness of the film used. So, is clear film the cheapest? Not necessarily. The thickness of the pouch is determined by how much material it will require/use. This plays the largest role in determining price, followed closely by the actual materials (aluminum foil, polyester metalized film, clear film, etc.) used in the different layers.

The advantages and disadvantages of three commonly used structures are noted here.

Clear Structures

Consider these advantages:

- ☐ You can see through them and/or print them with a clear window.
- ☐ Excellent barrier properties are available.
- ☐ Strong, puncture-resistant film structures are available.
- ☐ There are many choices based on the use and needs of the client.
- ☐ Cost effective (not always the cheapest, depending on the overall thickness and the other layers chosen). Clear is always cost effective.

And these disadvantages:

- ☐ You can see through it. (What's an advantage to some is a disadvantage to others.) Some clients choose a clear structure based on what they're packaging, their cost structure, the style of pouch, etc. If the product to be packaged is sensitive to light, we will under-print the pouch with a solid color to make it opaque and prevent light from affecting the product(s) inside.
- ☐ If you are printing this pouch and/or printing everything except a "clear window" area, consider under-printing the rest of the pouch (except the clear window area). This may add a minimal amount to the price per piece. However, if this isn't done, the printing will look translucent, drab, dull, and boring.

Metalized Film Structures

Metalized film is not foil (aluminum). Rather, it's usually made from polyester and is only one layer of the overall structure.

Consider these advantages:

- ☐ Opaque (doesn't allow light into the product inside)
- ☐ Because of this opacity, the printing naturally "pops" without the need to under-print.
- ☐ Excellent barrier properties available.
- ☐ Cost effective

- ☐ Strong, puncture-resistant structures available. Lots of combinations available depending on your criteria.

And this disadvantage:

- ☐ Opaque (can't see through to the contents inside)

Aluminum Foil Structures

Consider these advantages:

- ☐ Opaque (doesn't allow light into the product inside)
- ☐ Because of this opacity, the printing naturally "pops" without the need to under-print.
- ☐ Strong, puncture-resistant structures available. Lots of combinations available depending on your criteria.

And these disadvantages:

- ☐ Tends to be more expensive than other structures.
- ☐ Doesn't flex...meaning once foil is folded the crease and "lines" stay there and can affect the look, and over time can affect the barrier properties of the film itself.

Some of this information pertains to the overall cost, some to print capability, some to the strength and durability required. This information can help you tremendously as you start this journey. As always, trust your packaging professionals to assist you as you navigate the road ahead. Counting on them will save you time, aggravation, and money.

FAQs for Mid-Market and Larger Firms

Mid-market companies have a completely different mindset and approach when it comes to printed stand up pouches or any type printed flexible barrier packaging for that matter. People in small companies are interested in the basics such as how to create artwork, how to match colors, how to build their brand or find the right size pouch for their particular product.

However, the larger mid-market firms generally know what they need. They have graphic designers and know what colors and materials work for their particular products. They are concerned directly with growth, speed, and the best service and price for what they're ordering.

(To be clear, it's not that speed and price aren't important to small companies—they certainly are. But they deal with smaller quantities than mid-market companies do, so the overall dollar cost isn't nearly as much.)

10 Questions for Mid-Market Companies

1. Can you keep up with my demand and production needs?
2. What makes StandUpPouches.net different than other suppliers?
3. If I'm happy with my current supplier, why should I choose your company?
4. How fast can you run my custom-printed stand up pouches?
5. Do you have Hot Rush options in case I'm in a jam and need product ASAP?
6. How do you ship my printed stand up pouches?
7. What additional quality steps do you take?
8. Can I make changes to my artwork?
9. I cannot afford to run out of packaging. What options do you have for supply chain and inventory management?
10. Can I use the same material that works best on my equipment?

Can you keep up with my demand and production needs?

Smaller companies are extremely concerned with such things as finding the right material to use, how to create their artwork, or determining the correct size, but mid-market companies are completely different. They are all about quantity, quality, price, and speed (*QQPS*). They know how to create their own artwork and what material works best on their equipment. They want to know if we not only can make what they want and need but if we can scale and ramp up with them. If they get that sudden order from Whole Foods or Target, can we keep up?

The answer to this question is a resounding YES! We are one of the few companies that can run small volume and trial orders to help mid-market companies try a new flavor or version. We can also ramp up and run hundreds of thousands—even millions—of bags at a time on the same equipment without a difference in quality. If a client needs something run domestically within 3 to 4 weeks, we can do that. If a client wants a lower cost and can wait longer, we can run at our overseas plant and deliver within 7 to 10 weeks. Either way, the print quality and packaging quality will match seamlessly.

Even further, we can create a supply chain program for our clients. That means we can always have inventory for them on hand 24-7 so they never run out. Or we can release inventory based on their projections. We would then run more product at our factory as needed and agreed upon and replenish the inventory.

We understand that our client companies "work their tails off" to get deals with major retailers. The last thing they can afford to do is run out of packaging. Our programs assure them we can keep up. But more than that, we can become a critical piece of their company's success.

What makes StandUpPouches.net different?

SQSQ does, of course! Scale. Quality. Size. Quantity.

Scale. We can scale and run your packaging as fast as your business runs. Do you need a trial run in 3 to 4 weeks, then need to ramp up and run 100,000 bags a few weeks later? We can do that. Did you suddenly get an order from that major retailer and need 1,000,000 bags urgently? Yep, we can deliver that, too. From 7,500 pieces to 750,000 bags and more, we've got you covered, all without compromising quality.

Quality. Our factories are ISO and QS14000 certified. We use FDA and food-grade films, non-leeching water-based inks, and films that are landfill friendly and sensitive to the environment. We have successfully worked with some of the largest brands in the world—not only in the United States but in the world—and we can help your company.

Speed. We have more than eight different printing machines, including Flexographic and Rotogravure. With them, we do more than make printed flexible packaging; we control the manufacturing process. If you need something put on a

Rotogravure printing machine on a "fast track" and turned around quickly, we can do that.

Quantity. As mentioned earlier, we have the unique ability to run small trial volumes to help our clients prove if a flavor or version works. We then run 10 or 100 times that quantity to meet a trade show or a new retailer deadline. Having the right quantity on hand can be the difference between getting an order or going out of business!

If I'm happy with my current supplier, why should I choose your company?

There are several aspects to consider in response to this question:

Margins. Whether you are packaging a food product, a pet treat, or liquid soap, you constantly get squeezed for margins. Globally, food prices and ingredients continue to climb; critical components are going up in price. Retailers are wielding more pressure on their suppliers for slotting fees and lower prices. Where can lower costs come from? Packaging. Our unique business model allows us to reduce packaging costs while increasing efficiency and supply chain effectiveness. We offer versatility, with our pouches being made either domestically or at our overseas factory. We will inventory and deliver packaging as needed from our Ohio warehouse, whether the packaging is produced in the United States or overseas. As a result, you'll save money and increase efficiency at the same time.

Domestic + Overseas Plants. Our domestic factory can make custom-printed stand up pouches and other styles of flexible barrier bags within four weeks—out the door and in your hands. If a client needs a quick turn-around, we'll do a run in our U.S. factory but then implement a supply chain solution by running a large quantity at our overseas factory. It has identical structures and printing but drastically lower prices. We hold this inventory in our Ohio warehouse and release it as you need it.

Supply Chain. A company's supply chain only works if you have material on hand; you simply cannot afford to run out of product! That's where we shine. We'll hold your products in our warehouse, release when you need it as often as you need it, and then replenish our stock to your agreed-upon inventory levels. While this seems simple, 85% of what kills orders (and ultimately relationships with major retailers) is not having product when they want it.

Back-up Supplier. Let's face it, machines can break down, employees can go on strike, and companies can get busy, pushing your order to the back of the line. Wouldn't it be comforting to have another supplier who wants your business? Even better would be if that company controlled the manufacturing at multiple factories. That way, if you need something in a hurry, you've got options.

Problem-solving. Problems happen. Your supplier gets comfortable with your orders and maybe you don't get the service and attention you deserve. Perhaps something goes wrong with your order, and your current vendor doesn't seem to care. With another supplier backing you up, you now have options.

Run Small Trial Orders. Would you appreciate a company that can run small trial orders customized and printed for your application? That way, you can run a small batch to ensure that everything works properly on your equipment with your contract manufacturer or packager. This service makes you feel comfortable about placing large orders down the road while minimizing your risk.

How fast can you run my custom-printed stand up pouches, either as a small trial run or a large volume?

Domestically, we can run custom-printed stand up pouches in 3 to 5 weeks, start to finish. This timeline begins after your artwork has been approved and includes developing the printing plates/cylinders/proofs and so on.

Overseas, we can run your order in 4 to 5 weeks after your artwork approval, not including time for shipping. For shipments that go via sea, it takes 7 to 10 weeks from after your artwork is approved until your order is delivered to your door.

Alternatively, we can ship via air from our overseas factory in about one week using a door-to-door service with a FedEx or UPS type of service. (It's not as expensive as you might think.) If your order is shipped by sea, plan 2 to 3 weeks for delivery. We ship to the West Coast of the U.S. and unload orders in Los Angeles. From there, we deliver orders to our West Coast clients. For clients in the Midwest and on the East Coast, we ship to Tacoma, Washington, by sea and then transport orders by railcar to our warehouse in Cleveland,

Ohio. Your pouches are often sent out the same day they arrive via LTL carrier.

Do you have Hot Rush options in case I'm in a jam and need product ASAP?

Yes, both of our factories, domestic and overseas, have Hot Rush capability. The key is knowing how many you need and when you need them. Often a client wants only a handful for a tradeshow or client meeting. In that case, we can run a small amount by digital printing press in a matter of days. These pouches are printed digitally and look as if they were made from a production line. However, once the film has been printed, the pouches will be formed and sealed by hand. They will be fully functional but not as strong and robust as if they were made from a production machine.

If a client needs more than a handful, we analyze Hot Rush lead times from both our domestic and overseas plant and provide two options. These will be production run without any restrictions as experienced with digital printing.

How do you ship my printed stand up pouches?

From our domestic factory, we ship LTL and full truckloads when needed. From our overseas factory, we ship to either the Port of Ningbo or Shanghai, where we have our own warehouse collect, inspect, then pack the freight into our own container. *This is important to emphasize.* Once our pouches arrive at our warehouse at the port, they are inspected so we know they are in good shape to ship. Then they're loaded into *our own 20- or 40-foot* steel container (not part of another company's container) which is locked, sealed, and processed for shipment. This lock and seal is not disturbed until it arrives at our Los Angeles or Ohio warehouses.

What additional quality steps do you take that no other company does?

Both of our factories, domestic and overseas, are ISO 9000 certified. However, our Asian factory goes even further to assure quality. Not only is it ISO 9001 and ISO 14001 certified, it uses outsourced independent testing labs such as:

- ☐ Intertek
- ☐ SGS
- ☐ Veritas

That means we can send samples of our pouches and have one of these laboratories examine them for food-grade film usage, cleanliness, puncture resistance, and strength. This step isn't necessary, but for those clients who want extra assurance, we are happy to do this. Using an independent lab does add cost to the client, but it is possible.

Can I make changes to my artwork?

Yes, in three different ways: before, during, and after production.

Before production: Once we receive your artwork file, we create an electronic proof. This proof confirms the size of pouch you want, places the artwork on the pouch as requested, and lists the various colors you want printed. You are free to make any changes you want at this time.

During production: This gets tricky, but it's possible. Once you have approved your artwork, we make your printing cylinders, which are etched and engraved metal rollers. Each color of your artwork requires one printing cylinder. We then place ink onto these cylinders and print a piece of film by hand. Called a film proof, it is not a finished pouch but rather a thin substrate to show the details of the artwork on film. On request, we can send you this film proof to review, and if you need something changed, we can still do it. Separate charges may be involved depending on how much is changed.

After production: Certainly, after production any changes can still be made. An advantage of Rotogravure printing is using printing cylinders, so even if you make lots of artwork changes, the only cylinders that need changed are specific colors. For example, say you changed all the ingredients and text on your pouch. Because the text is in black, the only cylinder that needs to be changed is the cylinder that prints black, or one cylinder. Our printing cylinders cost between $225 and $250 per cylinder.

I cannot afford to run out of packaging. Do you offer inventory management and supply chain solutions?

Plain and simple, we don't run out of product. As mentioned, we have warehouses on the West Coast, in Ohio, and overseas. That gives us the ability to offer inventory programs both domestically and overseas in a seamless way.

For example, we can have your products stored at our overseas factory as well as at our Ohio warehouse. Once we release your order from our Ohio warehouse, we replenish the quantity from our overseas warehouse and start a new order to restock your pouches.

Further, we can work off of forecasts of future orders and deliver printed stand up pouches wherever and whenever you want them—daily, weekly, monthly, or quarterly. These shipments can go right to your factory or to your outsourced production facility.

Can I use material that works best on my equipment, or do I need to use your specified material?

If you have a material you've used successfully on your equipment and want us to supply it for you, no problem. We can have our domestic factory or our overseas factory make it for you to your exact specifications. If you would like to explore new materials that may work even better, we can provide short runs of product for you to try.

GLOSSARY FOR FLEXIBLE PACKAGING MATERIALS

You may think this is TMI (too much information) but now that you know everything about creating a knockout, custom-printed stand up pouch, here are some technical terms you can throw around.

Abbreviation	Generic Name/Common Trade Name
BOPP	*biaxially-oriented polypropylene*
BON	*biaxially-oriented nylon*
EVA	*ethylene-vinyl acetate*
EVOH	*ethylene-vinyl alcohol*
LDPE	*low-density polyethylene*
LLDPE	*linear low-density polyethylene*
OPP	*oriented polypropylene*
PET	*poly(ethylene terephthalate)*
PLA	*poly(lactic acid)*
PP	*polypropylene*
PS	*polystyrene*
PVDC	*poly(vinylidene chloride)*

FLEXIBLE PACKAGING TERMS

air gap

The distance from the die lips of a polymer-melt extruder and the chill roll.

anilox roll

Engraved ink metering roll used in flexo presses to provide a controlled film of ink to the printing plates that print onto the substrate.

aluminum foil

A thin-gauge (.285-1.0 mil) aluminum foil laminated to plastic films to provide oxygen, aroma, and water vapor barrier properties.

baggy, bagginess

(a) In processing flexible packaging materials, slack areas in the web that should be flat. Usually caused by bands of unequal thickness (gauge bands) in the rollstock.

(b) A roll in which the tension is not even across the width of the roll. A slack floppy area in the web is caused by the material being stretched and permanently elongated in the tighter areas. Rolls of film or laminate where one side of the material coming off the roll is loose or baggy while the opposite edge is tight is said to have a baggy edge.

barrier

In packaging, this term is most commonly used to describe the ability of a material to stop or retard the passage of atmospheric gases, water vapor, and volatile flavor and aroma ingredients. A barrier material is one that is designed to prevent, to a specified degree, the penetrations of water, oils, water vapor, or certain gases as desired. Barrier materials may serve to exclude or retain such elements without or within a package.

base film

The original form in which a film exists before coating or laminating.

biaxial orientation

Orientation of plastic films in both machine and cross-machine (transverse) directions by stretching. Biaxial stretched films are generally well balanced in both directions and are much stronger in terms of tear strength.

bleed

Image or color that extends beyond the trim edge of the finished printed piece.

burst strength

A measure of the ability of a sheet to resist rupture when pressure is applied to one of its sides by a specified instrument under specified conditions.

butt

(a) To join with, overlap, or space between.

(b) Butt register is where two or more colors meet with no significant overlap or space between.

cast film

Plastic film produced from synthetic resins (such as polyethylene) by the cast process. In this process, the molten resin is extruded through a slot die onto an internally cooled chill roll.

chemical resistance

Ability of a material to retain utility and appearance following contact with chemical agents. Chemical resistance implies that there is no significant chemical activity between the contacting materials.

chemical compatibility testing

Any procedure that exposes a material to chemicals or mixtures of chemicals to determine whether such exposure has a negative effect on the material being evaluated.

co-extrusion (COEX)

Simultaneous extrusion of two or more different thermoplastic resins into a sandwich-like film with clearly distinguishable individual layers.

COF (coefficient of friction)

Coefficient of friction, a measurement of "slipperiness" of plastic films and laminates. Measurements are usually done from film surface to film surface. Measurements can be done to other surfaces as well, but this is not recommended, because COF values can be distorted by variations in surface finishes and contamination on test surface.

coating

Any fluid material applied as a thick layer to a substrate material or object.

color management

The process of translating specific color information from the computer screen image, through prepress, plate-making, printing presses, and finally to a substrate in such a manner that color accuracy is maintained at acceptable levels throughout.

color value

The lightness or darkness of a color. A color may be classified as equivalent to some member of a series of shades ranging from black to white. The other two fundamental characterizers of color are hue and saturation.

compatibility

The ability of a container or material to resist chemical degradation or physical change caused by the product, or where a container or material does not chemically degrade or physically change the contained product.

corona treatment

A treatment to alter the surface of plastics and other materials to make them more receptive to printing inks.

cross-linking

A film conversion technique in which polymer chains are bound into a web or network to increase the web's heat stability and strength.

co-monomer

A monomer that is mixed with one or more other monomers for a polymerization reaction to make a copolymer.

curtain coating

A method of applying wax or other coating to a material where the material is passed through a free-falling curtain or film of the fluid coating.

cut edge

The uncovered edge of a laminated product. For example, a high-barrier paper/foil laminate made into a hermetically-sealed carton using lap seals would have an exposed cut edge of paperboard through which oxygen could still permeate into the product. Such edges are often skived and folded back on themselves to seal the cut edge.

cutoff

In web-fed processing, the cut or print length corresponding to the circumference of the plate cylinder.

deck

A term used mostly in flexographic printing to describe a single print station with plate, impression cylinders, and inking rolls.

degradation

A change or break-down in a material's chemical structure.

delamination

Separation or splitting of laminate layers caused by a lack of or inadequate adhesion, or by mechanical disruption such as peeling or shearing forces.

directionality

The tendency for certain materials to have properties imparted by the flow direction through a machine.

dot gain

A physical and/or optical measurement and theoretical calculation of the apparent increase in dot area from one medium to another. Normally expressed as the difference between a midtone (nominal 50%) dot area on a film negative and the printed dot area; for example, a 50% film dot area which prints as a 78% dot has 28% dot gain. Dot gain (and loss) are normal and must be controlled throughout the press and printing process.

draw

In flexible packaging laminates, the distance that a web travels between supporting rolls.

drawdown

A swatch of color or coating made by spreading a small amount of ink or varnish across a sheet of material. Made for visual comparison to a standard color swatch or chip.

ethylene acrylic acid (EAA)

EAA is a copolymer of ethylene and acrylic acid. Its ionic nature allows for excellent adhesive bonding to metal foil and other polar surfaces. EAA's adhesive and toughness qualities are taken advantage of in high-performance, multi-layer laminates.

ethylene-ethyl acrylate (EEA)

The copolymerization of ethylene with ethyl acrylate produces an ethylene acid copolymer. The polymers are produced with varying percentages of acrylate content, most typically between 15% and 30%. EEA is compatible with all olefin polymers and often is blended with these to modify properties. EEA is used in hot-melt formulations. It also can be used alone or as a component of heat-sealable coatings, where it offers improved toughness at low temperatures, excellent adhesion to nonpolar substrates, and a broad service temperature range. EEA is used as a tie layer between mating laminate films.

ethylene-methyl acrylate (EMAC)

The copolymerization of ethylene with methyl acrylate produces an ethylene copolymer, one of the most thermally stable of the olefin copolymers. The polymers are produced with varying percentages of methyl acrylate content, most typically between 18% and 24% of the structure. Alone or in blends, it has found applications in film, extrusion coating, sheet, laminating, and co-extrusion.

ethylene-vinyl acetate (EVA)

A polar copolymer of ethylene and vinyl acetate, retaining some of the properties of polyethylene but with increased flexibility, elongation, and impact resistance. EVA is frequently specified as the extrusion coating on polypropylene, aluminum foil, and poly(ethylene terephthalate) to provide good heat-seals at high converting rates, or as the adhesion layer in some laminates.

ethylene-vinyl alcohol (EVOH)

Can be regarded as a copolymer of polyethylene in which varying amounts of the -OH functional group have been incorporated. A typical packaging EVOH is about 20% to 35% ethylene. EVOH is one of the best polymeric oxygen barriers available to packagers. However, its susceptibly to water requires that for most applications it be laminated or co-extruded into a protective sandwich with materials that will keep the EVOH layer away from water.

extrusion

The process of forming a thermoplastic film, container, or profile by forcing the polymer melt through a shaped orifice.

extrusion coating

A process wherein a film of molten polymeric material is extruded onto the surface of a substrate material and cooled to form a continuous coating.

extrusion lamination

A laminating process in which individual layers of multi-layer packaging materials are laminated to each other by extruding a thin layer of molten synthetic resin (such as polyethylene) between the layers.

eye-mark register

A printed rectangular mark most often found along the edge of webstock that can be identified by an electric eye. The mark identifies a point on the web where an individual package is to be cut.

film

Generally used to describe a thin plastic material usually not more than 75 micrometres (0.003 inch) thick.

finishing

Any final operation done to packaging before shipping.

fitment

A device attached to the container finish to provide a performance function. For example, a pour-out fitment is plastic component for a glass, plastic, or metal package, designed to improve the dispensing action of liquid products.

flexible packaging

A package or container made of flexible or easily yielding materials that, when filled and closed, can be readily changed in shape. A term normally applied to bags, pouches, or wraps made of materials ranging in thickness from 13 to 75 micrometres (0.0b0á to 0.003 inch) such as paper, plastic film, foil, or combinations of these.

flexographic printing

A method of printing using flexible rubber or photopolymer printing plates in which the image to be printed stands out in relief. Fluid ink metered by an engraved roll is applied to the raised portions of the printing plate and then transferred to the substrate.

form-fill-seal (FFS)

A packaging machine that forms, fills, closes, and seals a package in one continuous or intermittent-motion operation. Flexible packaging stock fed from a roll is folded to the desired package shape and stabilized by heat sealing. The product is placed into the formed package, and the remaining opening is sealed. Machines can be configured so that the stock travels horizontally through the machine (horizontal form-fill-seal) or vertically through the machine (vertical form-fill seal).

four-color process

Printing with cyan, yellow, magenta, and black ink (CMYK) using halftone screens to create a full-color reproduction.

four-side-seal pouch

A pouch with seals along all four edges. Four-side-seal pouches can be made from a single stock, or the front and back can be different stocks. The pouches are most commonly made on multilane pouch-forming machines where 16 or more pouches can be placed across the width of the web.

gas chromatography

An instrumental method of accurately determining the composition of volatile solvents and oils, as well as their residual presence in materials such as laminates or plastics.

gas transmission rate (GTR)

The quantity of a given gas passing through a unit area of the parallel surfaces of a film, sheet, or laminate in a given time under the test conditions. Test conditions may vary and must always be stated.

gauge band

A thickness irregularity found in rolls of film. A thicker area in the machine direction at some location across the width of a flat film will produce a raised ring in a finished roll. Gauge bands can cause winding problems and, when unwound, the material tends not to be perfectly flat.

gauge

Thickness. In North America, film thickness, measured in mils, is usually given in gauges. A 100 gauge shrink film is one mil, or 1/1000 of an inch, thick. In Europe, the film thickness metric is the micron. A quick equivalency equation is: 1 mil = 25.4 microns.

good manufacturing practice (GMP)

Good manufacturing practice implies that the entire manufacturing procedure has been designed in such a way as to produce a quality product that presents a minimum risk to the consumer. GMP will vary from industry to industry depending on the nature of the product being packaged. Many GMPs have been formalized and are required by law for critical industries such as food and pharmaceutical packaging. Typically these GMPs describe the kind of equipment to be used, its validation, manufacturing procedures, inspection types and frequencies, record keeping, container types and approvals, and registration of company and product.

gravure printing

Gravure is abbreviated from the term rotogravure. During gravure printing an image is etched on the surface of a metal cylinder and is chrome plated for hardness. The ink fills the cells and is transferred onto the printing substrate.

gusset

The fold in the side or bottom of the pouch, allowing it to expand when contents are inserted

HDPE

High-density (0.95–0.965) polyethylene. Has much higher stiffness, higher temperature resistance, and much better water vapor barrier properties than LDPE, but it is considerably hazier.

heat-seal coating

An adhesive coating applied to a packaging material that is capable of being activated by heat and pressure to form a bond.

heat-seal layer

A heat-sealable innermost layer in plastic packaging films and laminates. Can be either adhesive laminated or extrusion coated onto a non-sealable film (or foil).

heat-seal strength

Strength of heat-seal measured after the seal is cooled (not to be confused with "hot tack"; see next item).

hermetic seal

Airtight or impervious to gases or fluids under normal conditions of handling and storage.

high barrier

Describes a material or package that has very low gas-permeability characteristics; that is, it offers a great deal of resistance to the passage of a gas through its volume.

hot tack

Strength of heat seal measured before the seal is cooled, which is very important for high-speed packaging operations.

impulse sealer

Also known as a heat sealer. These units use an electrical current passed through a Ni-Chrome wire heating element to seal bags and tubing. Can be used on many plastic materials to create strong permanent welds.

laminate

(a) *noun* A product made by bonding together two or more layers of material.

(b) *verb* To unite layers of material to produce a multilayer material.

laminated film

An adhered combination of two or more films or sheets made to improve overall characteristics. Also, multi-layer film.

lap seal

A seal made with two layers of film overlapping one another. Because lap seals require less material than fin seals, packagers are converting to lap seals in the name of sustainability, lean operations, and economics.

laser scoring

Use of high-energy narrow light beam to partially cut through a material in a straight line or shaped patterns. This process is used to provide an easy-opening feature to various types of flexible packaging materials.

LDPE

Low-density (0.92–0.934) polyethylene. Used mainly for heat-seal ability and bulk in packaging.

lidding, lidstock

Material or stock used to form a lid. For example, material that can be heat-sealed over the open ends of pharmaceutical tablet blister cards.

light resistance

The ability of material to withstand exposure to light (usually sunlight or the ultraviolet part of the light spectrum) without change of color or loss of physical and/or chemical properties.

LLDPE

Linear low-density polyethylene. Tougher than LDPE and has better heat-seal strength, but has higher haze.

machinability

The ability of a film to run on packaging equipment.

machine direction (MD)

The direction that film moves through the packaging equipment.

manufacturing tolerance

Permissible variations from rated or marked capacities or dimensions established by standards or specifications for those.

MDPE

Medium-density (0.934–0.95) polyethylene. Has higher stiffness, higher melting point, and better water vapor barrier properties.

metalize

Applying a thin coating of metal to a nonmetallic surface by chemical deposition or by exposing the surface to vaporized metal in a vacuum chamber.

MET-OPP

Metalized OPP film. It has all the good properties of OPP film, plus much improved oxygen and water vapor barrier properties, but not as good as MET-PET.

MET-PET

Metalized PET film. It has all the good properties of PET film, plus much improved oxygen and water vapor barrier properties. However, it is not transparent. See also VMPET.

moisture vapor transmission rate (MVTR)

A depreciated term, usually measured at 100% relative humidity, expressed in grams/100 square inches/24 hours (or grams/square meter/24 Hrs). See WVTR.

Mylar®

Mylar is a registered trademark of the DuPont-Teijin corporation. It is the industrial brand name for that corporation's polyester (PET) film. Polyester film is a staple of multi-layer packaging for a wide variety of applications.

neoprene

A synthetic chlorinated butadiene rubber used to make flexographic rollers resistant to alcohols, Cellosolve, water, aliphatic hydrocarbons, and esters.

nylon

Polyamide resins, with very high melting points and excellent clarity and stiffness. Two types are used for films: nylon-6 and nylon-66. The latter has much higher melt temperature, thus better temperature resistance, but the former is easier to process and is cheaper. Both have good oxygen and aroma barrier properties, but they are poor barriers to water vapor.

off-cut

Trim that is not utilized. In flexible packaging, a narrow roll of material left over when a material order does not call for the full roll width. Sometimes called a butt roll.

OPP

Oriented PP (polypropylene) film. A stiff, high-clarity film, but not heat sealable. Usually combined with other films (such as LDPE) for heat sealability. Can be coated with PVDC (polyvinylidene chloride) or metalized for much improved barrier properties.

optics

The visual properties of a film, such as clarity, gloss, haze, opacity, etc.

orientation

The process of mechanically stretching plastic film or parts in order to produce a straightening and alignment of the molecules in the stretch direction. If done in one direction, the material is said to be uniaxial or monoaxially oriented. If done in two directions, the film is biaxially oriented.

*OTR*Oxygen transmission rate. Varies considerably with humidity, therefore it needs to be specified. Standard conditions of testing are 0%, 60%, or 100% relative humidity. Units are cc/100 square inches/24 hours (or cc/square meter/24 Hrs). (cc = cubic centimeters)

pass

One trip of a material through a production machine or manufacturing step.

pillow pouch

A bag or pouch in the form of a tube that is sealed at both ends. Pillow-type pouches are most commonly produced on vertical-form-fill-seal (VFFS) machines and are characterized by seals across the top and bottom and a longitudinal seal going down the center of one of the faces.

plate break

Non-print area where the two ends of flexo plate butt together after being wrapped around the plate cylinder on the printing press.

PMS Number

The Pantone Matching System is the universally accepted color definition system. Colors can be blended or individually specified to match a specified Pantone reference color exactly.

polyethylene film (PE)

Made in high-density, low-density, linear low-density, and metallocene variations. By far the largest volume packaging film family.

poly(ethylene terephthalate) film (PET)

Polyester (Polyethylene Terephtalate). Tough, temperature-resistant polymer. Biaxial-oriented PET film is used in laminates for packaging where it provides strength, stiffness, and temperature resistance. It is usually combined with other films for heat sealability and improved barrier properties.

polyolefin

Family name for the polymers (plastics) derived by ethylene and propylene, such as polyethylene (PE) and polypropylene (PP).

polypropylene film (PP)

Unoriented film is soft and clear but brittle at low temperatures. This property as well as stiffness, strength, and clarity are improved by orientation.

pouch

A small bag usually constructed by sealing one or two flat sheets along the edges. There is no clear distinction between a pouch and a sachet other than the common understanding that a sachet is smaller.

primer coat

A coating applied over a substrate for the purpose of improving an ink or adhesive bond.

process color

Color printing created by separating the copy into the primary colors to produce individual halftones of each color that are then recombined at the press to produce the complete range of colors of the original. Process -printed photographic reproduction would normally be done with cyan, magenta, yellow, and black (CMYK) inks.

PVDC

Polyvinylidene chloride. A very good oxygen and water vapor barrier, but not extricable, therefore it is found primarily as a coating to improve barrier properties of other plastic films (such as OPP and PET) for packaging. PVDC-coated and saran-coated are the same.

register

Exact alignment of one part or operation with another part or operation.

release coating

A coating applied to the non-sealing side of cold-sealable packaging films and laminates supplied in a roll form that will allow the packer to unwind these films or laminates on packaging machines.

retort

The thermal processing or cooking of packaged food or other products in a pressurized vessel for purposes of sterilizing the contents to maintain freshness for extended storage times. Retort pouches are manufactured with materials suitable for the higher temperatures of the retort process, generally around 121° C.

reverse printing

Printing wrong-reading on the underside of transparent film. In this case, the outermost layer is printed on the backside and laminated to the rest of the multi-layer structure. While not mandatory in all industries, it is the preferred method for the food industry as it guarantees there will be no ink contact with the food product. The majority of all products are reverse printed.

roll stock

Refers to any flexible packaging material that is in a roll form.

slip

The ability of film to move easily over hard plastic, metal, or ceramic platforms or against another piece of film.

slitting

The conversion of a given width of a film or sheet material into narrower widths. Web stock is unrolled past a series of knives set to the correct widths, and the slit web is rewound back into roll form.

splice

Joining two pieces of web material to form a continuous web.

spot color

Solid colors not created by using screens. Usually a Pantone Matching System (PMS) color.

stand up pouch

A flexible pouch design where the bottom portion has been gusseted in such a way that that it provides a wide enough base of support so the pouch is able to stand up for display or use.

stick pack

A narrow flexible packaging pouch commonly used to package single-serve powder beverage mixes such as fruit drinks, instant coffee, and tea, as well as sugar and creamer products.

stickyback

Double-faced adhesive-coated material used for mounting elastomeric printing plates to the plate cylinder.

surface print

A process whereby the ink is deposited directly onto the outermost surface of the packaging film or material. The process is most commonly used in short-run printing. A UV (ultraviolet) coating may be added to provide a hard exterior finish that prevents the ink from flaking or chipping.

tear resistance

The ability of a film to resist the propagation of a tear.

tensile strength

The amount of pull a film can withstand without tearing apart or stretching.

thermoforming

A method of forming plastics wherein a plastic sheet is heated to a point where it is soft and formable.

threading

The placing of a web material through the various rolls and stations of any web-fed press such as a printer or laminator in preparation for production.

three-side-seal pouch

A pouch that is formed by folding the web material into a U shape and then sealing the three open sides. The pouch may be made with a gusseted bottom. Three-side-seal pouches are typically made on horizontal form-fill-seal machines.

tie layer

A material that bonds two incompatible layers in a coextrusion.

transverse direction (TD)

The direction perpendicular to the machine direction.

trapping

In printing, inks may be overlapped slightly by increasing the image size to ensure that no substrate shows through within the register variations of the printing press.

tunneling

A laminating defect caused by incomplete bonding of the substrates.

unit-dose package (UDP)

A pharmaceutical package that holds individual items of use. A complete unit-dose package may hold a number of discrete items, but each unit of use must be released individually from the package, generally in a non-resealable manner.

vapor barrier

A layer of material through which water vapor will pass only slowly or not at all.

void

An emptiness or absence of a substance. For example, an area of coated film that is not coated.

water vapor transmission rate (WVTR)

A measure of the rate of water vapor transmission through a material. Usually measured at 100% relative humidity, expressed in grams/100 square inches/24 hours (or grams/square meter/24 Hrs). See MVTR.

web

A continuous length of paper film, foil, or other flexible material as it is unwound from a roll and passed through a machine.

zipper pouch

A flexible plastic pouch with a molded-in-place sealing device wherein a projecting rib or fin is inserted into a mating channel to effect a closure. A zipper seal can be repeatedly opened and closed.

ACKNOWLEDGMENTS

I would like to express my gratitude to the professionals who have been instrumental in the successful completion of this project: Debbie Weil of Voxie Media (book coach and publisher); and Barbara McNichol and Tim Lawrence (non-fiction editors). Thank you all for your persistence and gentle guidance in helping me complete this book.

To my incredible wife, Susan: Thank you for believing in me despite all the crap I get us into.

To my kids, Emily and Spencer: Thanks for inspiring me to strive toward my full potential so I can be a great example for you.

To my business partner, Tammi Olle: You amaze me with your dedication and support. Thank you for all you have done and continue to do.

Finally, to my mother, Barbara: You said I wouldn't amount to anything, and for the longest time I tried to prove you right. Thank you for inspiring me to reach higher.

ABOUT THE AUTHOR

David Marinac is founder and CEO of ABC Packaging Direct and StandUpPouches.net and a 30-year veteran of the custom-packaging industry. He helps businesses succeed through custom-printed flexible packaging that is irresistible to customers and that also grows their brand.

His revolutionary approach combines cutting-edge Internet marketing techniques, a powerful virtual team, unmatched customer service, and a can-do-anything attitude.

Over the past ten years, he has built StandUpPouches.net into the leading online brand for flexible packaging. His company now sells over ten million pouches annually, with sales doubling year after year.

WHAT TO DO NEXT

1. Go to **www.standuppouches.net** and request FREE samples.
2. Read our blog: **www.standuppouches.net/blog**
3. Search for 'standuppouches' and follow us:

4. Contact me at **dmarinac@standuppouches.net** or directly at 216-373-1005 for a free, fully-customized quote on your packaging project.